THE ANCIENT ROMAN —WORLD—

STUDENT STUDY GUIDE

Oxford University Press, Inc., publishes works that
further Oxford University's objective of excellence
in research, scholarship, and education.

Oxford   New York
Auckland   Cape Town   Dar es Salaam   Hong Kong   Karachi
Kuala Lumpur   Madrid   Melbourne   Mexico City   Nairobi
New Delhi   Shanghai   Taipei   Toronto

With offices in
Argentina   Austria   Brazil   Chile   Czech Republic   France   Greece
Guatemala   Hungary   Italy   Japan   Poland   Portugal   Singapore
South Korea   Switzerland   Thailand   Turkey   Ukraine   Vietnam

Copyright © 2005 by Oxford University Press, Inc.

Published by Oxford University Press, Inc.
198 Madison Avenue, New York, NY 10016
www.oup.com

Oxford is a registered trademark of Oxford University Press

All rights reserved. No part of this publication may be reproduced,
stored in a retrieval system, or transmitted in any form or by any means,
electronic, mechanical, photocopying, recording, or otherwise,
without the prior permission of Oxford University Press.

ISBN-13: 978-0-19-522159-6

Writer: Scott Ingram
Editor: Lelia Mander
Project Director: Jacqueline A. Ball
Education Consultant: Diane L. Brooks, Ed.D.
Design: designlabnyc

Casper Grathwohl, Publisher

Printed in the United States of America
on acid-free paper

Dear Parents, Guardians, and Students:

This study guide has been created to increase student enjoyment and understanding of *The Ancient Roman World*. It has been developed to help students access the text. As they do so, they can learn history and the social sciences and improve reading, language arts, and study skills.

The study guide offers a wide variety of interactive exercises to support every chapter. Parents or other family members can participate in activities marked "With a Parent or Partner." Adults can help in other ways, too. One important way is to encourage students to create and use a history journal as they work through the exercises in the guide. The journal can simply be an off-the-shelf notebook or three-ring binder used only for this purpose. Some students might like to customize their journals with markers, colored paper, drawings, or computer graphics. No matter what it looks like, a journal is a student's very own place to organize thoughts, practice writing, and make notes on important information. It will serve as a personal report of ongoing progress that your child's teacher can evaluate regularly. When completed, it will be a source of satisfaction and accomplishment for your child.

Sincerely,

Casper Grathwohl
Publisher

This book belongs to:

_____

CONTENTS

How to Use the Student Study Guides to *The World in Ancient Times*   6

Graphic Organizers   8

Important Vocabulary Words   10

Chapter 1   11
Wives, Wolves, and Wild Boys: The Founding of Rome
   There are two legends about the founding of Rome. Both show that Romans believed gods interacted with humans and changed their lives.

Chapter 2   13
Migration, Mystery, and Mastery: Who Were the Etruscans?
   Several groups came from different places to the Italian peninsula. Among these groups were the Italic peoples, the Greeks, and the Etruscans.

Chapter 3   15
Morality, Tyranny, Heroes, and Kings: The Beginnings of the Republic
   In 509 BCE, the Roman Republic, with consuls and lawmakers, was created.

Chapter 4   17
The Rebellion of the Poor: Class Conflict and the Twelve Tables
   Arguments between workers and wealthy landowners resulted in new laws.

Chapter 5   19
Fathers, Gods, and Goddesses: Religion in Ancient Rome
   Roman government and religion were closely related to the family organization.

Chapter 6   21
Hannibal, Rome's Worst Enemy: The Battle for the Mediterranean
   Roman victory in two wars against the North African empire of Carthage allowed the Republic to win control of the area around the Mediterranean Sea.

Chapter 7   23
A Roman Through and Through: Cato and Greek Culture
   Cato was a real leader in Rome who spoke out against the influence of Greek culture.

Chapter 8   25
Spartacus the Rebel: Slavery in Ancient Rome
   Slaves played an important role in the Roman economy and in Roman society.

Chapter 9   27
Two Revolutionary Brothers: The Gracchi and the Decline of the Republic
   The efforts of two brothers to create a more equal society caused violence between wealthy and poor Romans. This weakened the Republic.

Chapter 10   29
Words Versus Swords: Cicero and the Crisis of the Republic
   Despite the efforts of Cicero to save the Republic, a civil war further weakened the government and led to its collapse.

Chapter 11   31
"I Came, I Saw, I Conquered": Julius Caesar and the Roman Triumph
   Julius Caesar became the leader of the Roman Empire.

Chapter 12   33
Power-Mad or Madly in Love? Cleopatra, Queen of Egypt
   Cleopatra's reign in Egypt was marked by strong relations with Roman rulers, which led to Egypt's decline and the rise of Octavian.

Chapter 13   35
The Emperor's New Names: The Reign of Augustus
   The long rule of Augustus Caesar brought a period of peace to the Roman Empire.

Chapter 14   37
Misery, Mistrust, Madness, and Murder: The Successors of Augustus

The four emperors who followed Augustus ruled over a period of bloodshed, violence, and revolt.

Chapter 15   39
Childhood and Marriage, Mothers and Matriarchs: Women and Children
Although women had fewer rights than men in Rome, they played an important role in Roman society.

Chapter 16   41
A City Tells Its Tale: Pompeii and the Roman House
The eruption of Mount Vesuvius destroyed two Roman cities, but the disaster preserved Roman life for archaeologists to study thousands of years later.

Chapter 17   43
All the Emperor's Men: Trajan and the Army
The Roman army played a significant military and economic role in the expansion of the Roman Empire.

Chapter 18   45
Pleasing the Rowdy Romans: Gladiators and Circuses
Popular entertainment for Romans featured competitions, fights, and cruelty.

Chapter 19   47
How to Get Rich in Rome: Business and Trade
As the Roman Empire expanded, trade routes were established and a merchant class of Romans arose.

Chapter 20   49
The Restless Builder: The Emperor Hadrian
Hadrian was a practical leader who believed in strong defenses, and he was an artist who admired other cultures.

Chapter 21   51
Magic and the Cults of the Near East: New Religious Ideas
Romans were superstitious and worshipped gods from other regions of the empire.

Chapter 22   53
Taxes and Tactics in the Provinces: Administering the Empire
The economy of the Roman Empire was based on a well-organized system of census and taxation under the control of local administrators.

Chapter 23   55
One God or Many? The Jews of the Roman Empire
The Jews, the only ancient people to worship a single god, struggled for religious freedom against the Roman emperors.

Chapter 24   57
From Jesus to Constantine: The Rise of Christianity
Over the course of three centuries, the spread of Christianity created enormous change in the Roman Empire.

Chapter 25   59
Rome's Power Slips Away: The Barbarians
The movement of barbarian tribes across the Rhine and Danube Rivers eventually led to the collapse of the Roman Empire.

Chapter 26   61
The Empire, Divided and Defeated: The Fall of Rome/Epilogue
The Roman Empire collapsed in 476 CE after two centuries of decline, but its legacy remains powerful in the modern world.

Reports and Special Projects   63

Library/Media Center Log   64

HOW TO USE THE STUDENT STUDY GUIDES TO
THE WORLD IN ANCIENT TIMES

The World in Ancient Times will introduce you to some of the greatest civilizations in history, such as ancient Rome, China, and Egypt. You will read about rulers, generals, and politicians. You will learn about scientists, writers, and artists. The daily lives of these people were far different from your life today.

The study guides to The World in Ancient Times will help you as you read the books. They will help you learn and enjoy history while building thinking and writing skills. They will also help you pass important tests and just enjoy learning. The sample pages below show the books' special features. Take a look!

Before you read

- Have a notebook or extra paper and a pen handy to make a history journal. A dictionary and thesaurus will help you too.

- Read the two-part chapter title and predict what you will learn from the chapter.

- Quotation marks in the margin show the sources of ancient writings. The main primary sources are listed next to the chapter title.

- Study all maps and photos. Read the captions closely. (This caption tells that the statue itself is a primary source. Artifacts are records of history, just like writings.)

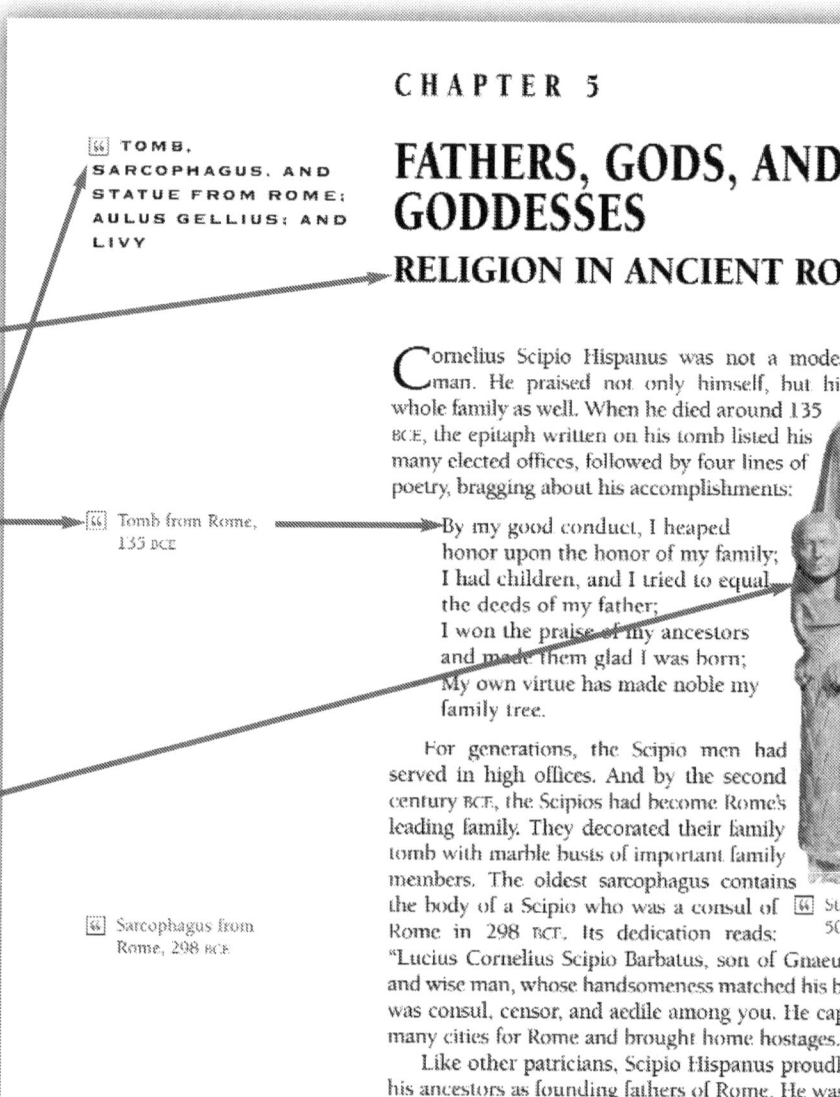

As you read

- Keep a list of questions.

- Note **boldfaced** words in text. They are defined in the margins. Their *root words* are given in *italics*.

- Look up other unfamiliar words in a dictionary.

- Find important places on the map on pp. 12–13.

- Look up names in Cast of Characters on pp. 9–11 to learn pronunciation.

- Read the sidebars. They contain information to build your understanding.

After you read

- Compare what you have learned with what you thought you would learn before you began the chapter.

FATHERS, GODS, AND GODDESSES | 37

looking at him. First: he's a Roman. We know because he's wearing a toga, the garment that was a sign of manhood. The Romans called it the *toga virilis,* and a boy wasn't allowed to wear it until he became a man, usually at 16. Second, because this unknown Roman is carrying masks of his ancestors, we know that his father or grandfather had served as one of Rome's top officials.

These masks, made of wax or clay, usually hung in the hallways of the ancestral home. Romans took them down and carried them in parades and funeral processions.

Roman families were organized like miniature states, with their own religions and governments. The oldest man in the family was called the **paterfamilias**, the patriarch. He was the boss, and his words were law. Scipio Hispanus was the paterfamilias in his family. This meant that he held lifelong power, even over life and death. He could sell or kill a disobedient slave. He had the right to abandon an unwanted baby, leaving him or her outside to die. Usually this would be a sick child or a baby girl to whom the family couldn't afford to give a dowry when she grew up. Romans wanted healthy sons to carry on the family name, yet a father could imprison, whip, disown, or even execute a son who committed a crime. In 63 BCE, a senator named Aulus Fulvius did exactly that after his son took part in a plot to overthrow the government. But this didn't happen very often. Roman fathers were expected to rule their families with justice and mercy, the same way that political leaders were expected to rule the state.

For both the family and the state, religion played a major role in life. Every Roman home had a shrine to the household gods, the Lares. The father served as the family's priest. Scipio Hispanus would have led his family's prayers and made sacrifices to honor their ancestors and please the gods that protected the entire family—living and dead. When a baby was born, Scipio Hispanus would have hit the threshold of his home with an axe and a broom to frighten away any wild spirits that might try to sneak in. When a household member died, family members carried the body out feet first to make sure that its ghost didn't run back inside. (That's why people still sometimes describe death as "going out feet first.")

vir = "man"
Roman boys donned the *toga virilis* when they became men. *Virilis* is a form of *vir;* "virile" means "manly."

pater + *familias* = "father" + "family"
The paterfamilias was the oldest male member of a Roman family.

TOMBS OF THE SCIPIOS

The Romans believed that the dead should neither be buried nor cremated inside the city walls. They were afraid that Rome's sacred places would become polluted by the presence of death. So they lined the roads leading away from Rome with monuments built to house and honor the dead. Visitors can still see the tombs of the Scipios buried along the Appian Way, about two miles from the Forum. (The Appian Way is a military road that was built in the fourth century BCE.)

The next two pages have models of graphic organizers. You will need these to do the activities for each chapter on the pages after that.

Go back to the book as often as you need to.

GRAPHIC ORGANIZERS

As you read and study history, geography, and the social sciences, you'll start to collect a lot of information. Using a graphic organizer is one way to make information clearer and easier to understand. You can choose from different types of organizers, depending on the information.

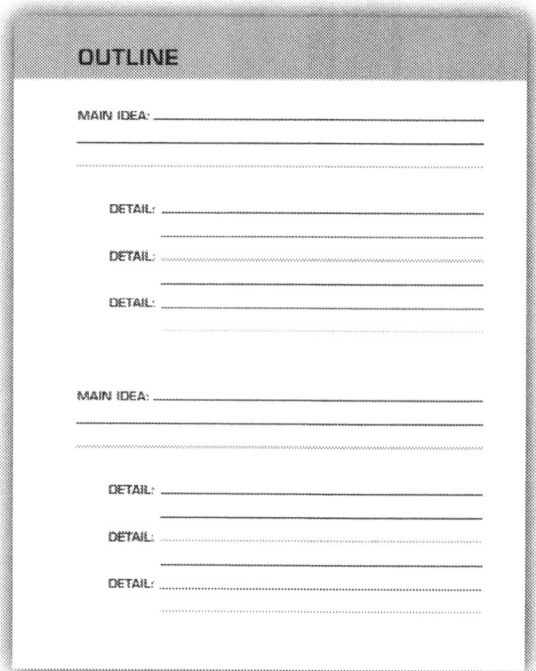

Outline
To build an outline, first identify your main idea. Write this at the top. Then, in the lines below, list the details that support the main idea. Keep adding main ideas and details as you need to.

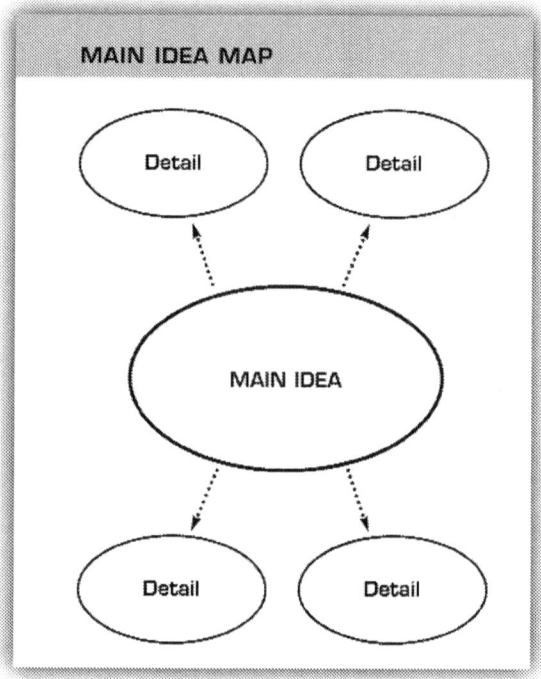

Main Idea Map
Write down your main idea in the central circle. Write details in the connecting circles.

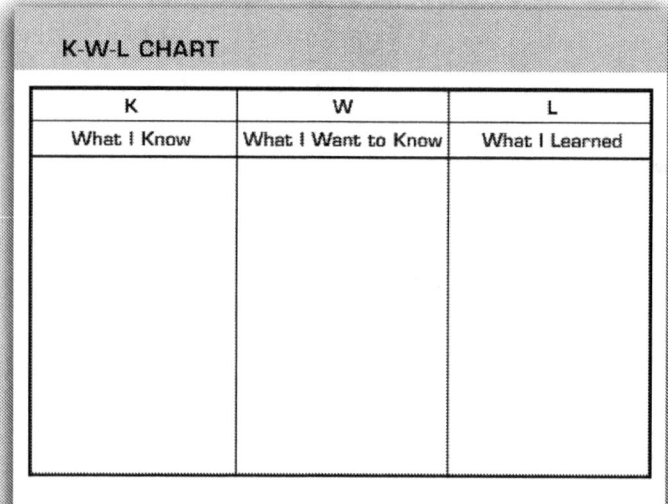

K-W-L Chart
Before you read a chapter, write down what you already know about a subject in the left column. Then write what you want to know in the center column. Then write what you learned in the last column. You can make a two-column version of this. Write what you know in the left and what you learned after reading the chapter.

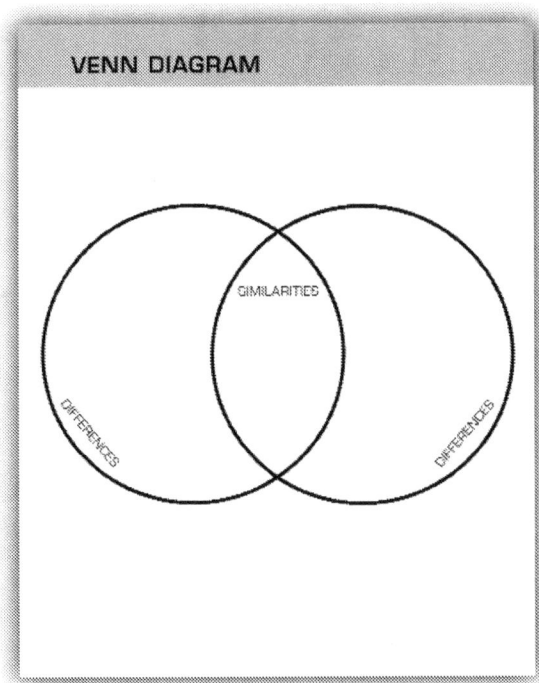

Venn Diagram

These overlapping circles show differences and similarities among topics. Each topic is shown as a circle. Any details the topics have in common go in the areas where those circles overlap. List the differences where the circles do not overlap.

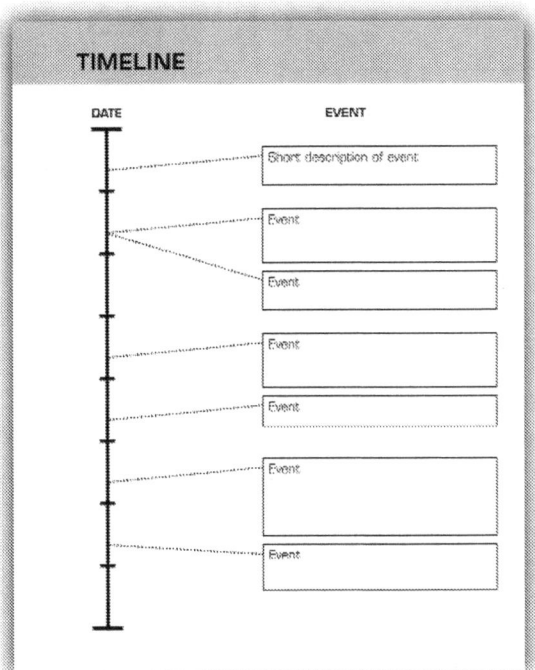

Timeline

A timeline divides a time period into equal chunks of time. Then it shows when events happened during that time. Decide how to divide up the timeline. Then write events in the boxes to the right when they happened. Connect them to the date line.

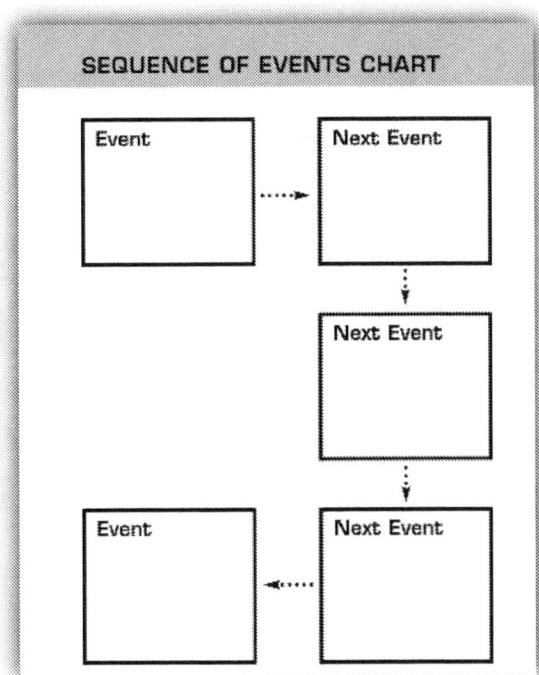

Sequence of Events Chart

Historical events bring about changes. These result in other events and changes. A sequence of events chart uses linked boxes to show how one event leads to another, and then another.

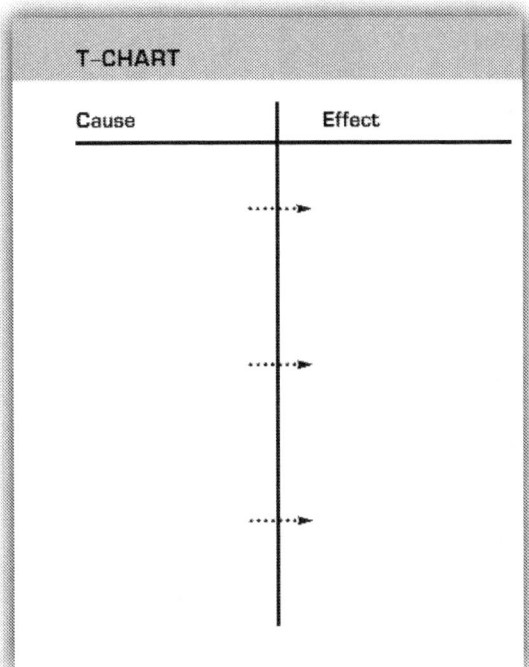

T-Chart

Use this chart to separate information into two columns. To separate causes and effects, list events, or causes, in one column. In the other column, list the change, or effect, each event brought about.

IMPORTANT VOCABULARY WORDS

The Word Bank section of each lesson will give you practice with important vocabulary words from the book. The words below are also important. They're listed in the order in which they appear in each chapter. Use a dictionary to look up any you don't know.

Chapter 1
divine
voyage
abandoned
divination
legend
eventually
truce
contradictory
mingling
cremate
archaeology
foundation

Chapter 2
immigrants
metalworkers
interconnecting
afterlife
colony
discoloration
sacrifice

Chapter 3
ruthless
solemn
condemn
exile
arrogant
magistrate
congratulate

Chapter 4
nourishment
status quo
discontented
decreed

Chapter 5
bust
sarcophagus
hostage
ancestral
procession

Chapter 6
seafaring
titanic
grappling
siege
demolish

Chapter 7
passionate
frugal
ruthless
scornfully
hindsight

Chapter 8
sketchy
fringe
auction

Chapter 9
oration
mushroomed
aristocrat
unruly
eligible
corrupt

Chapter 10
pompous
conceited
disdained
recruit
cooperate

Chapter 11
bizarre
omen
soothsayer
boundary
legion
lieutenant
brine
placard
embankment

Chapter 12
fluent
sibling
smuggled
pacify
extravagant
oblivious
undisputed
Ptolemaic
fatal

Chapter 13
resolution
triumphal
cutthroat
triumvir
decapitated
landgrab
turmoil
network
voluntarily
proclaim

Chapter 14
polio
sullen
grudgingly
malicious
traitor
lenient
grandeur
thrifty
bankrupt
conspiracy

Chapter 15
orator
epitaph
exasperating
fugitive
relief sculpture

Chapter 16
gymnasium
lavatory
disintegrate
graffiti
denarii

Chapter 17
cavalryman
legionary
century
centurion
discipline
wield
tactics
makeshift
predecessor
auxiliary
chain mail
citizenship

Chapter 18
mingle
tantalizing
gory
uproarious
groom
artificial
agility

Chapter 19
prominent
gratitude
investment
capsize
summon
infantryman
artifact
peddler
caravan
monsoon

Chapter 20
strenuous
sniper
villa
relic
catacombs
consecration

Chapter 21
pregnancy
misfortune
evil eye
astrology
meteorite
self-mutilation
depiction

Chapter 22
haven
tyranny
bristle
census
technology

Chapter 23
diaspora
persecute
suspicious
extremist

Chapter 24
prophet
Messiah
disciple
sermon
parable
missionary
martyr
bishop
incentive

Chapter 25
massacre
kinsman
flattery
ambush
underestimate
disorganized
catapult
cannibalism
dull witted
crucial
hordes
nomadic
ransack
traumatic
beggar

Chapter 26
humble
reorganize
tetrarchy
devastate
vulnerable
manufacture
adapt

Epilogue
ambassador
cement
concrete
tangible
civic

CHAPTER 1
WIVES, WOLVES, AND WILD BOYS: THE FOUNDING OF ROME

CHAPTER SUMMARY

There are two legends about the founding of Rome. Both show that Romans believed gods interacted with humans and changed their lives.

ACCESS

A legend is a special kind of story. What legends do you know, maybe about your hometown or your family? Do you think legends are always true?

BUILDING BACKGROUND

In your history journal, write down five beliefs Romans had about the way their city came to be.

CAST OF CHARACTERS

State why each character was important.

Aeneas (ay-NEE-us) _____

Romulus (ROM-yuh-lus) _____

Remus (REE-mus) _____

WHAT HAPPENED WHEN?

Write what happened on the date.

753 BCE _____

Read the sidebar *The Founding of a City* on page 15. Write a sentence that defines the term *founding*.

_____

WORD BANK

immortal

To live forever is to be _____.

WORD PLAY

The prefix *im-* sometimes means "not." What word describes a being that does not live forever?

_____

THE ANCIENT ROMAN WORLD

CRITICAL THINKING
CAUSE AND EFFECT

Draw a line from each cause and connect it to the result, or effect. (There is one extra effect.)

CAUSE	EFFECT
1. Amulius feared he would be overthrown,	a. they floated down the river and were saved by a she-wolf.
2. Rhea Silvia broke her vows,	b. the Romans and Sabines went to war.
3. A servant couldn't kill the babies,	c. Romulus killed Remus.
4. Remus made fun of Romulus,	d. Romans and Sabines called a truce.
5. Romulus's men kidnapped Sabine women,	e. Romulus and Remus were born.
6. The Sabine women ran onto the battlefield,	f. he forced Rhea Silvia to join the Vestal Virgins.
	g. Remus killed Romulus.

WITH A PARENT OR PARTNER

When you have completed the chart, read aloud each cause-and-effect pairing to a parent or partner. Use the word *so* to connect each cause with each effect.

WRITE ABOUT IT

The Trojan women were *appalled* that Aeneas and the Trojan men were planning another journey after they reached the mouth of the Tiber River. To be *appalled* means to be

a) happy.

b) excited.

c) shocked.

Circle your answer.

In your history journal, write a short dialogue or a descriptive scene between the Trojan men and women about making this second journey. Why were the women appalled? How did the men respond?

WORKING WITH PRIMARY SOURCES

The image at left is an ancient Roman coin. It shows an image of a Roman god. Think about what we can learn about ancient cultures through artifacts like this one. Answer the following questions in your history journal.

1. Why do you think the figure is wearing an olive wreath?
2. Why would the Romans put a god on their coins?
3. What famous people do we use on coins today? (It's okay to take a peek at your pocket change!)
4. If people found your coins hundreds of years from now, what conclusions might they draw about your culture?
5. Think up a design for your own coin and draw it in your history journal.

CHAPTER 2
MIGRATION, MYSTERY, AND MASTERY: WHO WERE THE ETRUSCANS?

CHAPTER SUMMARY
Several groups came from different places to the Italian peninsula. Among these groups were the Italic peoples, the Greeks, and the Etruscans. When people move from one place to start a new life in another place, we say they *migrate*.

ACCESS
Timelines help us see how events in history are connected. As you read the chapter, use the lines below to write what happened on certain dates. Then start make a timeline in your journal. Make marks every 25 years. (Use the model on page 9 to help you.)

TIMELINE
1000 BCE _____
 900 BC _____
 750 BCE _____
 616 BCE _____
 509 BCE _____

WHAT DO YOU KNOW?
Write three sentences about the Etruscans.
_____
_____
_____

CAST OF CHARACTERS
Etruscans (ee-TRUSS-kihns) _____

Did You Know? Today, the northern region of Italy is named after the Etruscans. It's called Tuscany.

WORD BANK
architect   omen   peninsula   immigrant   reservoir

Choose words from the Word Bank to complete the sentences. One word is not used at all. (Clue: Remember, we use *a* before words beginning with a consonant. We use *n* before words beginning with a vowel.)

1. Land bounded by water on all but one side is a _____.
2. A person who comes from one place to live in another place is an _____.
3. A person who designs buildings is an _____.
4. An _____ foretells the future.

THE ANCIENT ROMAN WORLD 13

WORD PLAY

Look up in a dictionary the word you did not use. Write a sentence using that word in your journal.

Which word in the word bank could be related to a word in the title of this chapter? _____
_____

ALL OVER THE MAP
MOVEMENT

Some people migrate, or move away, because they want to escape from a bad situation. You could say they are *pushed* out of their old home. Some people migrate because things are better in another place. You could say they are *pulled* toward a new home.

Make two main idea maps to explain why the Etruscans, Greeks, and Italic peoples migrated to Italy. Use the model on page 8 of this workbook for help. In the center of one, write *pull*. In the center of the other, write *push*. Fill in words from the Word Bank below that are reasons for being pushed from an old home or pulled toward a new home. (Go back to the book or use your dictionary if you don't know a word.)

WORD BANK

war   hunger   wealth   land   freedom   poverty   drought

WORKING WITH PRIMARY SOURCES

The Etruscans, called Lydians by the historian Herodotus, left their country because of a bad situation. Read the sentence below to learn about how they coped with their problem.

> The plan . . . against the famine was to engage in games one day so . . . as not to feel any craving for food, and the next day to eat . . . [and] abstain from games.

Circle the word in the first sentence that means "a long period without food."

WRITE ABOUT IT

Imagine taking care of a younger child. You have to think up ways to take the child's mind off food. Write down in your history journal some ways of keeping people from thinking about eating.

WITH A PARENT OR PARTNER

Imagine that you are an Etruscan child in ancient Rome. Reread the chapter and think about what it would be like to live in Rome in those days. What would you do with your time? What would your parents do? Copy the t-chart from this study guide (see page 9) into your history journal. Label one column *Etruscan Life*. Label the other column *My Life Today*. Get together with a partner from school or a parent at home and fill out the columns to compare your life today with that of a child in ancient Italy.

CHAPTER 3
MORALITY, TYRANNY, HEROES, AND KINGS: THE BEGINNINGS OF THE REPUBLIC

CHAPTER SUMMARY

In 509 BCE, the Roman Republic, with consuls and lawmakers, was created.

ACCESS

Think about the differences between a monarchy and a republic. What type of government do we have in the United States? What are the advantages of this type of government?

WHAT DO YOU KNOW?

In your history journal, copy the K-W-L chart from page 8 of this book. In the first column, write everything you know about republics. (If you don't know anything, that's okay.) In the next column, write down what you want to find out. Go back to this chart after finishing the chapter and write notes in the final column, *What I Learned*.

CAST OF CHARACTERS

Write the names of the characters below in a column in your history journal. As you read the chapter, write short sentences about why each person was important.

Tarquin (TAR-kwin)

Brutus (BROO-tus)

Horatius (huh-RAY-shee-us)

Cincinnatus (SIN-suh-nah-tus)

Lucretia (loo-KREE-shuh)

WHAT HAPPENED WHEN?

509 BCE _____
475 BCE _____
458 BCE _____
266 BCE _____

Make a timeline in your history journal of the dates and events above.

WORD BANK

Senate   citizens   republic   Assembly   consuls   dictator   aedile   magistrates   praetor   tyrant

Choose words from the Word Bank to complete the sentences. One word is not used at all. Go back to the book to check information.

1. Problems with the city waterworks were handled by an _____.
2. Officials or _____ could not serve for more than two years in a row.
3. Farmers who had a disagreement over property rights went before a _____.
4. The _____ handled all of the money that came into the treasury.
5. When the rule of kings was ended, power was held by two _____.
6. The _____ was made up of all the landowning men, who were _____.
7. The change in government from monarchy to _____ took place after Tarquin was forced from power.
8. A _____ could hold absolute power in an emergency.

Look up in a dictionary the word you did not use. Write a sentence using that word.

CRITICAL THINKING

Who did what in the Roman Republic?

Complete the chart below by checking the boxes that apply.

	men	absolute power	appointed official	highest official elected
Senate	☐	☐	☐	☐
Assembly	☐	☐	☐	☐
consul	☐	☐	☐	☐
dictator	☐	☐	☐	☐
magistrate	☐	☐	☐	☐

One column should be checked top to bottom. Write a sentence about what this means about who had the power in Rome and who did not. _____
_____
_____

WORKING WITH PRIMARY SOURCES

From *Parallel Lives*, by Plutarch (c. 100 CE)

> Brutus . . . was of a severe and inflexible nature. . . . he let himself be so [filled] with . . . hatred against tyrants, that, for conspiring with them, he proceeded to . . . execut[e] . . . his own sons.

Flexible means "able to be bent." What does *inflexible* mean? What other word meaning "harsh" is similar to *Brutus*? (Use a dictionary or thesaurus for help.) _____
_____
_____

WITH A PARENT OR PARTNER

An editorial shows a writer's opinions. With a parent or partner, find an editorial in your local newspaper. Then in your history journal, write an editorial for *The Roman Times* titled "A Great Leader." Choose one of these starters:

1. "A great leader must be feared and fierce."
2. "A great leader must be flexible and understanding."

You can use information about Brutus or Cincinnatus from the book, or other leaders you know. Be sure to include two reasons to support your claim.

CHAPTER 4

THE REBELLION OF THE POOR: CLASS CONFLICT AND THE TWELVE TABLES

CHAPTER SUMMARY

Arguments between workers and wealthy landowners resulted in new laws.

ACCESS

Think of the rules at your school and the laws in your town. Think about who makes these rules and laws. This chapter explains how Roman laws came to be.

The sequence of events chart (model on page 9 of this workbook) is a good way to understand Chapter 4. In the first box, write "Plebeians stopped work and left Rome." Fill in the boxes that follow as you connect events. The result box should contain a fact from the final paragraph of the chapter.

CAST OF CHARACTERS

Write why Agrippa was important.

Agrippa (uh-GRIP-uh) Menenius (men-EN-ee-us) _____
_____
_____

WHAT HAPPENED WHEN?

493 BCE _____

450 BCE _____

DO THE MATH

How many years passed between the two events? _____
_____

WORD BANK

patrician   rebellion   *status quo*   tribune   veto   plebeian

Fill in the paragraph with words from the Word Bank.

In about 483 BCE, a conflict arose between two classes of Romans. On one side was the wealthy _____ class. On the other side was the poor working _____ class. When the workers refused to work, the Roman leader Agrippa Menenius convinced them to return to their jobs. But the workers did not to go back to the _____. They were angry about the way things had always been. As a result, the Senate agreed to give the workers the right to elect _____ to represent them in the government. These elected workers had the right to _____ laws that they did not agree with. Eventually, a set of laws was passed. This gave rights to rich and poor citizens of Rome.

THE ANCIENT ROMAN WORLD   **17**

WORD PLAY

Look up in the dictionary the word that you did not use. Write that word in a sentence.

_____

What two words would be a good title for this paragraph? (Hint: One of the words is a number.)

_____

CRITICAL THINKING
COMPARE AND CONTRAST

Plebeians and patricians did different jobs in ancient Rome. Sort the list of activities by each group in the graphic organizer below.

| serve as soldiers |
| work in fields |
| lead troops |
| make sandals |
| collect taxes |
| weave cloth |
| pass laws |
| sell fish |
| own land |
| load wagons |
| build temples |

Patrician	Plebeian

WORKING WITH PRIMARY SOURCES

The Roman Code of Law

Below are laws from Table 8 of the Twelve Tables.

- If one has broken a bone of a freeman with his hand or with a [club], let him pay a penalty of three hundred coins.
- If one has broken the bone of a slave, let him pay one hundred and fifty coins.
- Any person who destroys by burning any building . . . shall be . . . put to death . . . [if] he committed the . . . misdeed with malice aforethought; but if he . . . committed it by accident . . . he [must pay for] the damage or, if he be too poor . . . he shall receive a lighter punishment.

MAKING INFERENCES

1. Do Romans value slaves and free Romans equally? Yes ____ No ____

    In your journal, write why you think so.

2. What does *malice* mean? Use your dictionary if you need help. Write a definition.

    _____

    _____

Fore is a prefix or a suffix that often means "earlier." Can you think of a word using *fore* that means "earlier"? _____

3. What do you think *malice aforethought* means?

    ____ a) Doing something good on purpose

    ____ b) Doing something bad on purpose

    ____ c) Doing something bad by accident

18 CHAPTER 4

CHAPTER 5
FATHERS, GODS, AND GODDESSES: RELIGION IN ANCIENT ROME

CHAPTER SUMMARY
Roman government and religion were closely related to the family organization.

ACCESS
What can you learn from the chapter title about religion in Rome? The K-W-L chart on page 8 of this book will help you get the most from Chapter 5. Copy this chart in your history journal. In the first column list five topics about family and religious life in Rome. In the second column, write what you want to learn about each topic. Fill in the third column with information about each fact as you read the chapter.

CAST OF CHARACTERS
Write why each of the characters was important.

Scipio (SIP-ee-oh) Hispanus (his-PA-nus) _____

Vestal (VES-tul) Virgins _____

WORD BANK
toga virilis   ancestor   paterfamilias   Lares   sarcophagus

Choose words from the Word Bank to complete the sentences. One word is not used at all. (Clue: We use *a* before words beginning with a consonant. We use *an* before words beginning with a vowel.)

1. Statues of an _____ who died years before often showed that person dressed in a _____.

2. A _____ in the Roman family acted like a priest when he led ceremonies to honor _____.

WORD PLAY
Look up in the dictionary the word that you did not use. Use that word in a sentence.
_____

Why is January, the first month of the year, named after the spirit with two faces—one looking forward and one looking back—known as Janus? _____
_____

THE ANCIENT ROMAN WORLD

CRITICAL THINKING
CLASSIFICATION

Romans believed in gods of many kinds. Some were household spirits, called the Lares. They helped with everyday things. Others were gods with great powers, such as Jupiter, the king of gods. They helped with big, important actions.

The words below describe things Romans might do or say when asking household spirits or powerful gods for help. Put them in the right column.

throw flour into a fire

pray for a good harvest   give thanks for victory

toss salt onto the hearth

carry masks in funerals   pray for help in ruling Rome

Household Spirits	Powerful Gods

IDENTIFYING MAIN IDEA

Complete the two sentences that explain the difference between household spirits and gods.

A spirit _____

A god _____

Read the second paragraph on page 38, about a family's daily offering. Why do you think "salt and flour symbolized the basic needs of life"? _____

_____

_____

WORKING WITH PRIMARY SOURCES

Polybius on Roman funerals, from *History* (146 BCE)

> When any [famous] person dies, he is carried . . . to the . . . forum; placed . . . in an upright posture . . . And while . . . people stand round, his son . . . [or relative] extols the virtues of the deceased, and . . . recalls his past actions. . . .

WRITE ABOUT IT

Choose a person from Roman history that you admire. In your journal, make a list of the things that person did or the qualities about him or her that you admire. Then write a speech you might deliver at the Forum. Read it aloud to a parent or partner.

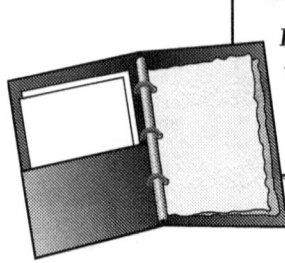

HISTORY JOURNAL

Don't forget to share your history journal with your classmates, and ask if you can see what their journals look like. You might be surprised—and get some new ideas.

CHAPTER 6

HANNIBAL, ROME'S WORST ENEMY: THE BATTLE FOR THE MEDITERRANEAN

CHAPTER SUMMARY

Roman victory in two wars against the North African empire of Carthage allowed the Republic to win control of the area around the Mediterranean Sea.

ACCESS

Graphic organizers help us remember important information. In your history journal, make a chart with three columns. In the first column, list the cast of characters. The second column should be called *What I Know*. The third column should be called *What I Learned*. In the second column, write everything you already know about each person. (If you don't know anything, that's okay.) After you read the chapter, in the last column write what you found out about each person.

CAST OF CHARACTERS

Identify the following people.

Hamilcar Barca (HAM-ul-kar BAR-kuh) _____

Hannibal _____

Scipio Africanus (SIP-ee-o af-ri-KAH-nus) _____

WHAT HAPPENED WHEN?

Use the blanks to fill in the events that took place on the dates below. Then in your history journal make a timeline, divided into five-year parts, from 270 BCE to 210 BCE.

264–241 BCE _____

218 BCE _____

217 BCE _____

WORD BANK

fertile   alliances   cavalry   ambushed   siege

Choose words from the Word Bank to complete the sentences. One word is used twice; one word is not used at all.

1. Soldiers on horseback form a military unit called a _____.
2. _____ soil is good for growing crops.
3. Armies in _____ don't have to fight alone.
4. The _____ was _____ when it was attacked by surprise.

Look up in a dictionary the word you did not use. Write a sentence using that word.

WORD PLAY

The core of a word is a smaller word or group of letters within the word. Looking at the core of a word can help you figure out what word means and build vocabulary. Can you think of another word that has the same core as *alliance*? Use the dictionary for help. Write the word and its definition in your journal.

THE ANCIENT ROMAN WORLD   **21**

CRITICAL THINKING
CAUSE AND EFFECT

Draw lines in the chart below to match the effect in the left column with the correct cause in the right column. (There is one extra cause.)

EFFECT	CAUSE
1. Carthage helped Syracuse	a. they had no navy.
2. Romans invented grappling hooks	b. they were in Italy for 10 years.
3. Hamilcar Barca went to Spain	c. he conquered Carthage.
4. Hannibal laid siege to Sagantum	d. Hannibal pretended to retreat.
5. Roman troops were trapped	e. Rome made an alliance with Sagantum.
6. Carthaginian troops became exhausted	f. Rome helped Messina.
7. Scipio received the title "Africanus"	g. Carthage needed copper and silver.
	h. they used elephants in battle.

WITH A PARENT OR PARTNER

When you have completed the chart, read aloud each cause-and-effect pairing to a parent or partner. Use the word *because* to connect each effect with each cause. Try to make a sentence using the extra cause.

ALL OVER THE MAP
INTERACTION

1. Messina is on the northeast tip of Sicily, and Syracuse is on the southeast tip of Sicily. Locate each city on the map with an "x" and a label. Compute distances between these cities using the scale. Write these distances on the map.
2. Draw a flag over the city that Hannibal placed under siege for eight months before it fell.
3. Mark Hannibal's battles on the map of Italy in the right order: Locate the first battle by writing "1," and so forth.
4. Circle the location of Hannibal's final battle.
5. Use shading or different patterns to mark Roman territory and and Carthaginian territory at 218 BCE. Then key these patterns in the legend.

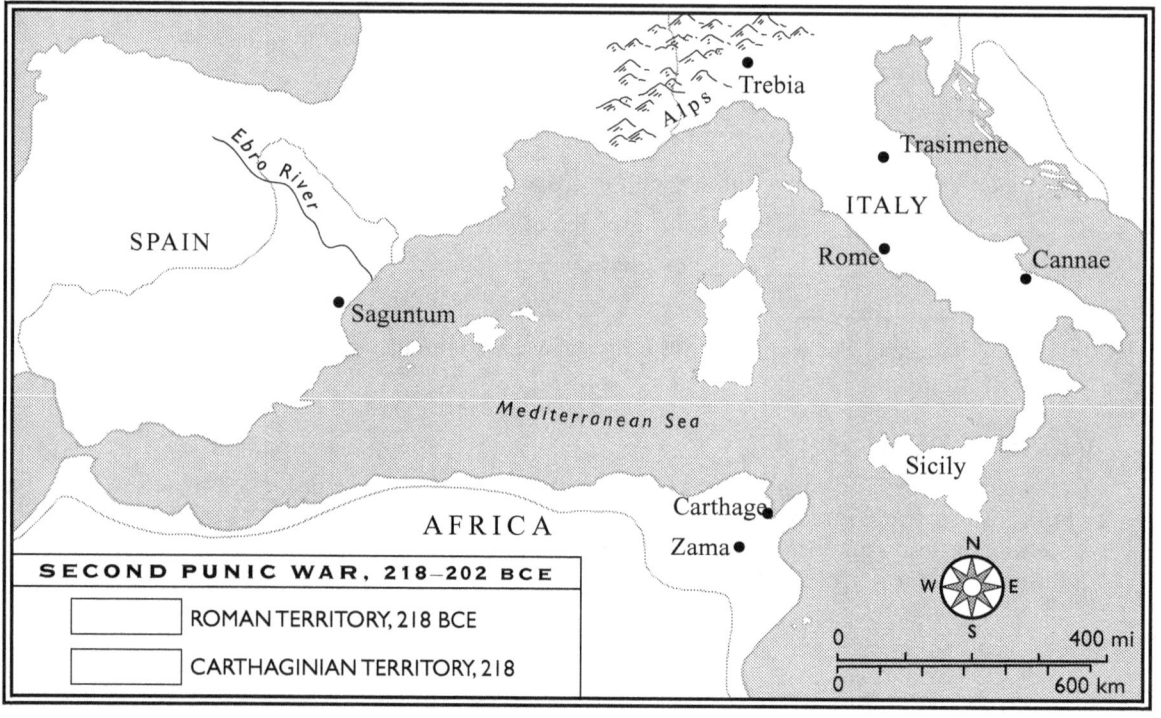

22   CHAPTER 6

CHAPTER 7
A ROMAN THROUGH AND THROUGH: CATO AND GREEK CULTURE

CHAPTER SUMMARY
Cato was a real leader in Rome who spoke out against the influence of Greek culture.

ACCESS
Cato had many of different talents. Copy the main idea map from page 8 of this workbook. In the largest circle write *Cato*. In each of the smaller circles, write one fact about Cato that you learn as you read the chapter.

CAST OF CHARACTERS
Write why these three characters are important.

Cato (KAY-to) _____

Alexander the Great _____

Antiochus (an-TIE-uh-kus) III _____

WHAT HAPPENED WHEN?
336 BCE _____

190 BCE _____

149 BCE _____

In your history journal, make a timeline with the dates and events. Use the timeline graphic organizer on page 9 of this workbook.

DO THE MATH
Did the year 336 BCE come before or after 190 BCE? _____

WORD BANK
remedies   aqueducts   oration   censor   empire   reign

Choose words from the Word Bank to complete the sentences. One word is not used at all.

1. The time during which a king rules over a country is called his _____.

2. A _____ watched over the behavior of people in Rome.

3. Romans used plants and animals as _____ for sickness.

4. A politician in Rome had to present his ideas in a powerful _____ to succeed.

5. Water was carried in Rome by _____.

THE ANCIENT ROMAN WORLD

WORD PLAY

Look up in a dictionary the word that you did not use. Write that word in a sentence.

_____

WITH A PARENT OR PARTNER

How many other words can you think of that begin with *aque* or *aqua*? Write them down in your history journal. What do they all have in common?

WORKING WITH PRIMARY SOURCES

Cato made a famous statement to contrast the Greeks and the Romans. He said:

"Greeks speak from the lips; Romans speak from the heart."

This type of statement is called an *adage*. Usually an adage is a short, simple expression. It uses symbolic language to make a general observation. Another example of an adage is the popular saying "Too many cooks spoil the broth." This expression means that when too many people are in charge of a project, they run the risk of spoiling it. What other adages do you know?

IDENTIFYING POINT OF VIEW

Think about the meaning of Cato's adage. Is it a compliment or a criticism of the Greeks? What does it say about the Romans? To help answer this question, reread the description of Cato on pages 47–48. In the space below, explain whether Cato approves or disapproves of the Greek way of life, and why he feels that way. _____

_____

_____

_____

IN YOUR OWN WORDS

Rewrite Cato's adage using different words and expressions. Follow the same format:

"Greeks _____; Romans _____."

WITH A PARENT OR PARTNER

Adages are general observations about human nature and daily life. They don't mean exactly what they say, but they use symbols and metaphors to make a point. Some examples of adages are:

- A stitch in time saves nine.
- A bird in the hand is worth two in the bush.
- Many hands make light work.

Working with a parent or partner, see if you can make up some adages of your own. Write them down in your history journal.

HISTORY JOURNAL

Don't forget to share your history journal with your classmates, and ask if you can see what their journals look like. You might be surprised—and get some new ideas.

CHAPTER 8
SPARTACUS THE REBEL: SLAVERY IN ANCIENT ROME

CHAPTER SUMMARY
Slaves played an important role in the Roman economy and in Roman society.

ACCESS
Slavery has been a terrible part of the history of many countries. In the United States, the Civil War was fought to end slavery. In Rome, slaves revolted. To organize information from this chapter, make a chart with two columns in your history journal. The first column should be called *What I Know*. Write everything you already know about slavery in ancient Rome. (If you don't know anything, that's okay.) The second column should be called *What I Learned*. After you read the chapter, write everything that you have learned about slavery in Rome.

CAST OF CHARACTERS
Write a sentence to describe each person.

Spartacus (SPAR-tuh-kus) _____

Crassus (KRASS-us) _____

Use your dictionary to find a word that has the same root as *Crassus*. Write that word's definition in your history journal.

WHAT HAPPENED WHEN?
135 BCE _____

73 BCE _____

WORD BANK
Choose words from the Word Bank to complete the sentences. One word is not used at all.

crucified   aristocrat   barracks   rebellion   freedman

1. A slave who took part in a revolt or _____ would be _____, or hung on a cross and left to die.

2. A person who was not a slave but also was not a member of the wealthy class was called a _____.

3. A free, wealthy male was known as an _____.

WORD PLAY
Look up in a dictionary the word that you did not use. Write that word in a sentence.

_____

What Latin word beginning with "p" might be used to describe a *freedman*? _____

What Latin word beginning with "p" might describe an *aristocrat*? _____

(Hint: check chapter 4)

THE ANCIENT ROMAN WORLD   **25**

WRITE ABOUT IT
WITH A PARENT OR PARTNER

Spartacus was a hero. What is a hero? In your journal, make a chart with two columns. In one column make a list of your heroes. In the other column write why each one is a hero to you. Ask a parent or partner to make the same chart and fill it in. Compare and discuss your choices of heroes.

CRITICAL THINKING
SEQUENCE OF EVENTS

The sentences below list events in the slave rebellion under Spartacus. Use numbers to put them in the correct order (use "1" for the first event, and so on).

_____ The rebels twisted vines into ropes and surprised the Romans.

_____ Crassus defeated the rebels and killed Spartacus.

_____ The rebels defeated Mummius.

_____ More than 6,000 rebels were crucified on the Appian Way

_____ Spartacus and his men stole kitchen knives and escaped.

_____ The rebels stole weapons and hid on top of Mount Vesuvius.

_____ More than 70,000 slaves joined the rebellion.

THINK ABOUT IT

Why did Crassus order the "appalling" execution of his own men before the final battle with Spartacus?

_____

_____

WORKING WITH PRIMARY SOURCES

Pseudolus, by Plautus (200 BCE)

Masters mistreated slaves in ancient Rome and elsewhere. In the play *Pseudolus* (pronounced SOO-doh-luss), the main character, Ballio, calls his slaves before him.

> Come . . . you rascals . . . kept at a loss, bought at a loss. Not one of you . . . of use to me, unless I carry on thus! (He strikes his whip.) . . . (To audience) All they do is . . . drink, eat, and [steal] . . . (To them) Now . . . [listen] to what I say. Take care that when I'm back from the Forum I find [the house] swept, smoothed, cleaned and set in order. Today's my birthday . . . I want to entertain some fine gentlemen in real style, to give the idea that I'm rich.

Circle words that give Ballio's opinion of household slaves. In your history journal, write two sentences comparing Ballio's treatment of slaves with the description given on page 57 in the book. Write what you think of Ballio, and then write what you think wealthy Romans might have thought of him.

GROUP TOGETHER

Wouldn't it be fun to know what other students think about slavery in ancient Rome? How does it compare to slavery in more recent times? Get a few friends together and ask your teacher to help you organize a discussion group at school. Have one person take notes and another person present the group's ideas to the class.

CHAPTER 9
TWO REVOLUTIONARY BROTHERS: THE GRACCHI AND THE DECLINE OF THE REPUBLIC

CHAPTER SUMMARY
The efforts of two brothers to create a more equal society caused violence between wealthy and poor Romans. This weakened the Republic.

ACCESS
Do you have brothers, sisters, or close relatives about your age? If so, in what ways are you alike? In what ways are you different? Tiberius and Gaius Gracchus were two brothers who brought changes to Rome. In your history journal, label one page *The Gracchi Brothers*. Make two columns, one labeled *alike*, the other labeled *different*. Fill in the columns as you read and learn about the brothers.

CAST OF CHARACTERS
Write a sentence about why each character was important.

Tiberius (ti-BEER-ee-us) Gracchus (GRAK-us) _____

_____

Gaius (GY-us) Gracchus (GRAK-us) _____

_____

WHAT HAPPENED WHEN?
Write what happened on each date below. Then make a timeline from the dates and events in your history journal.

133 BCE _____
123 BCE _____
 90 BCE _____

WORD BANK
Mediterranean Sea   importance   infuriated   revolutionary   *populares*   decline

Choose words from the Word Bank to complete the paragraph. One word is not used at all.

Romans believed that power and money brought them _____. Some Romans, however, were _____ by the powerful. They turned to the Gracchi brothers, who brought a _____ idea of leadership to the people. Under the Gracchi, the _____ spoke for the rights of the people and the Republic began to expand. By the end of the Gracchi reign, Roman cities were located around the _____, a body of water once known as "Our Sea."

THE ANCIENT ROMAN WORLD

WORD PLAY

Look up in a dictionary the word that you did not use. Write that word in a sentence.

___

Write any words in English you can think of that come from *populus*, the Latin word for "people."

___

CRITICAL THINKING
MAIN IDEA AND SUPPORTING DETAILS

Each sentence in *italics* below states a main idea from the chapter. Put a check mark in the blanks in front of all of the sentences that support or tell more about the main idea.

1. *The Gracchi brothers were noblemen whose family was well known in Rome.*
   _____ (a) Their father served two terms as a consul, the highest office in Rome.
   _____ (b) When Tiberius gave a speech, he spoke quietly and never moved from one spot.
   _____ (c) Their mother, Cornelia, was the daughter of the general Scipio Africanus, who had defeated Rome's great enemy, the Carthaginian general Hannibal.

2. *Rome was suddenly rich and powerful. But it was also suddenly full of problems.*
   _____ (a) Thousands of unemployed men hung around on the streets of the city, hoping to find work.
   _____ (b) Many had lost their jobs to foreign slaves, who didn't have to pay for labor.
   _____ (c) Still, they devoted themselves to improving the lives of the poor.
   _____ (d) Others in the street crowds were poor farmers whose land had been bought by wealthy aristocrats.

ALL OVER THE MAP
REGIONS

This map shows the territory that Rome gained from 241 to 44 BCE. Using the information below, add patterns or shading to the map to show what territory was added when. Then shade the boxes of the legend to match your shading on the map.

Roman territory in 241 BCE: Italy, Sicily, Sardinia, Corsica

Roman territory in 146 BCE: Spain, Macedonia, Greece, Carthage and surrounding territory in Africa

Roman territory at Caesar's death, 44 BCE: Gaul, Bithnynia, Cyprus, Syria

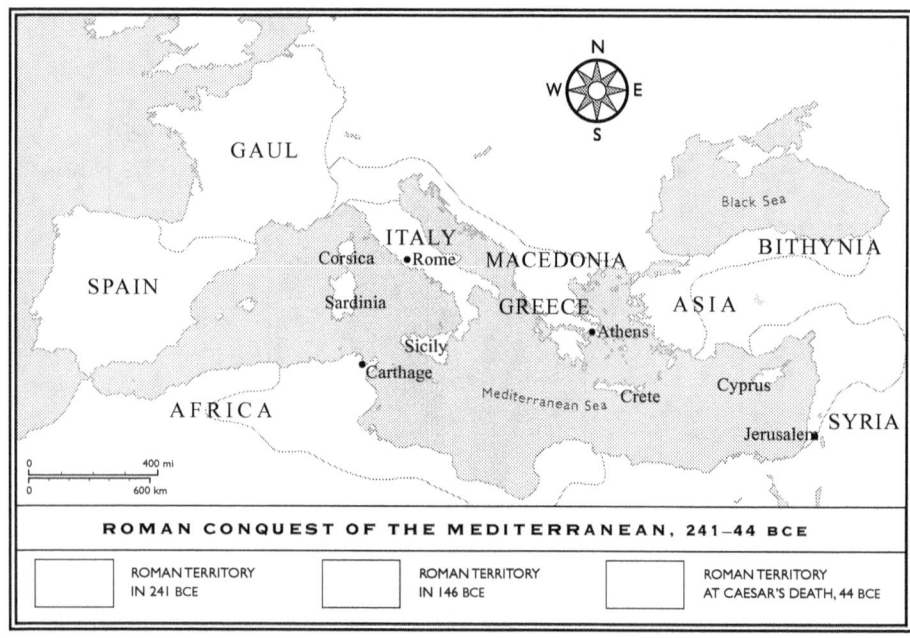

ROMAN CONQUEST OF THE MEDITERRANEAN, 241–44 BCE

| ROMAN TERRITORY IN 241 BCE | ROMAN TERRITORY IN 146 BCE | ROMAN TERRITORY AT CAESAR'S DEATH, 44 BCE |

CHAPTER 10
WORDS VERSUS SWORDS: CICERO AND THE CRISIS OF THE REPUBLIC

CHAPTER SUMMARY
Despite the efforts of Cicero to save the Republic, a civil war further weakened the government and led to its collapse.

ACCESS
George Washington is known as the father of his country because he was the first United States president. Cicero is called the father of Rome because he did a lot for the Roman Republic. Imagine that you could interview Cicero. Before reading, skim through the chapter. Then in your history journal make a list of five questions you would ask Cicero. One question might be "What is your opinion of the plebeians?" Now read the chapter carefully and write the answers to the questions as you imagine Cicero might answer them.

CAST OF CHARACTERS
As you read, write down two adjectives that would describe each character below. Then write why you chose it.

	Adjective	Why?
Cicero (SIH-sir-o)		
Pompey (PAHM-pee)		
Julius Caesar (SEE-zer)		
Mark Antony		

WORD BANK
innate   civil   orator   triumvirate   ruthless

Choose words from the Word Bank to complete the paragraph. One word is not used at all.

Cicero was a skilled _____, known for his powerful speeches. His writing ability seemed _____, as though he had been born with it. Unfortunately, the "father of his country" became a victim of the _____ wars between generals. The wars led to the fall of the Republic and the first _____.

THE ANCIENT ROMAN WORLD

WORD PLAY

Look up in a dictionary the word that you did not use. Write that word in a sentence. Then look it up in a thesaurus. Find an *antonym*, a word that means the opposite. Now rewrite your sentence using the antonym. _____

_____

WITH A PARENT OR PARTNER

In your history journal, list all the English words you can think of that begin with the same first syllable as *triumvirate*. Ask a parent or family member or partner to make a list, too. What does *tri* mean?

WHAT HAPPENED WHEN?

Write what happened on each date below.

75 BCE _____

63 BCE _____

43 BCE _____

CRITICAL THINKING
FACT OR OPINION?

A fact is a statement that can be proved. An opinion judges things or people, but it cannot be proved or disproved. Make a two-column chart in your journal. Label one column *Fact* and the other column *Opinion*. Write each sentence below from the chapter in the column where it belongs.

1. "Everyone in first-century Rome knew . . . Cicero's name."
2. "Many of Cicero's speeches and essays have also survived."
3. "Pompey paid no attention to Cicero's words."
4. "He (Cicero) is honored today as a man of genius . . ."
5. "Cicero was a snob."
6. "Cicero wasn't a coward."
7. "[H]e was in the right place at the wrong time."
8. "Cicero's voice was silenced. . . ."

WORKING WITH PRIMARY SOURCES

An essay on friendship by Cicero (44 BCE)

An essay is a type of writing that shows how a writer's personal opinion about one single subject. Read the second sentence in the first paragraph on page 67. Then read the sentences below from Cicero's essay.

> What can be more delightful than to have some one to whom you can say everything with the same absolute confidence as to yourself? In the face of a true friend a man sees . . . a second self. . . .

WRITE ABOUT IT

In your history journal, write a short essay about a character from this chapter. Imagine this person were a special friend. Explain how this friend is a "second self." Describe the qualities you admire in this person.

CHAPTER 11: I CAME, I SAW, I CONQUERED: JULIUS CAESAR AND THE ROMAN TRIUMPH

CHAPTER SUMMARY

Julius Caesar became the first ruler of the Roman Empire.

ACCESS

Julius Caesar was a person with many sides. He wasn't perfect. But he was a great leader who overcame a serious illness called epilepsy to rule the Roman Empire. In your history journal, copy the main idea map graphic organizer from page 8 of this workbook. In the largest circle, write *Caesar*. In the smaller circles write facts that you learn about Caesar as you read the chapter.

CAST OF CHARACTERS

Write a sentence about why each other character is important.

Pompey (PAHM-pee) _____

Julia _____

Brutus _____

WORD BANK

military

Look up the word *military* in the dictionary. Use it in a sentence.

_____

Now find the sentence on page 74 that uses this word. Rewrite the sentence using the definition instead of the word itself.

_____
_____

WHAT HAPPENED WHEN?

Write the events that happened on the dates below.

60 BCE _____
48 BCE _____
44 BCE _____
March 15, 44 BCE _____

TIMELINE

Make a timeline. Use the model on page 9 and mark off the years for 100 BCE to 40 BCE in 10-year segments. Place the dates above and the dates from chapter 10 on your timeline, with an explanation of what happen ed on each date during those important years.

Numbers Challenge: Read the sidebar *Math, Roman Style* on page 75. Write the dates of your timeline using Roman numerals. _____

COMPREHENSION
SEQUENCE OF EVENTS

The pairs of words below describe events in Caesar's life. Write *before* or *after* in the blank to complete each sentence correctly.

1. Caesar was declared dictator for life _____ he was assassinated in the Senate.
2. Caesar became the governor of Gaul _____ he formed the First Triumvirate.
3. The First Triumvirate ended _____ Caesar crossed the Rubicon River.
4. Caesar defeated Pompey's army in Greece _____ he followed Pompey to Egypt.
5. Caesar put Cleopatra on the throne _____ he defeated Ptolemy XIII.
6. Caesar wrote "*veni, vedi, vici*" _____ he returned to Rome.
7. A coin with Caesar's image was minted _____ his assassination.
8. Caesar said "You too, my son?" to Brutus _____ he was stabbed.
9. Rulers of Rome took the name *Caesar* _____ his death.

WORKING WITH PRIMARY SOURCES

Life of the Defiled Caesar, **by Suetonious** (130 CE)

Read the caption about Caesar on page 73. Then read the description of Caesar below.

> Caesar is said to have been tall, fair, and well-built, with . . . dark-brown eyes. His health was sound apart from . . . nightmares which troubled him . . . [and] he twice had epileptic fits while on campaign. He was something of a dandy, always keeping his head carefully trimmed and shaved. His baldness was a disfigurement which his enemies harped upon, much to his exasperation; but he used to comb the thin strands of hair forward . . . and of all the honors voted him . . . none pleased him so much as the privilege of wearing a laurel wreath on all occasions—he constantly took advantage of it.

MAKING INFERENCES

Answer the following questions in your history journal. Circle any words in the description to help you remember important things.

1. Why does Suetonius say that Caesar is "said to have been tall, fair, and well built" instead of "Caesar was tall, fair, and well built"? (Hint: When did Caesar die? When did Suetonius write?)
2. What does the word "dandy" mean, used this way?
3. Why is Caesar's baldness called a "disfigurement"? How did Caesar cover up his baldness?

WRITE ABOUT IT

Imagine that you are a visiting Rome from a distant city and Caesar happens to ride by. In your journal, write a letter to a friend describing your impression of the famous Roman leader. Begin like this:

My dear _____ (think up the name of Roman boy or girl):

The gods smiled on me today. I saw Caesar himself pass by. He rode _____. He wore _____.

He looked _____.

Add as many details as you can think of from the reading.

CHAPTER 11

CHAPTER 12
POWER-MAD OR MADLY IN LOVE? CLEOPATRA, QUEEN OF EGYPT

CHAPTER SUMMARY
Cleopatra's reign in Egypt was marked by strong relations with Roman rulers, which led to Egypt's decline and the rise of Octavian.

ACCESS
Do you ever read magazines that tell about where your favorite stars were seen and with whom they were seen? Cleopatra was a kind of star. She was seen with several famous people. Copy the main idea map on page 8 of this workbook in your history journal. In the first box, write *Historical Setting* with *Cleopatra* and the year she took the throne, *51 BCE*. Some of the people listed in the **Cast of Characters** are important to the story, and the years in **What Happened When** will tell you which events are important. Fill the rest of the boxes as you read through the chapter.

CAST OF CHARACTERS
Write a sentence explaining why each person was important.

Cleopatra (klee-o-PA-tra) _____

Mark Antony _____

Octavian (ok-TAVE-ee-un) _____

WORD BANK
consort   ancestor   pharaoh

Choose words from the Word Bank to complete the sentences. One word is not used at all.

1. The ruler of Egypt was called a _____ instead of *king* or *emperor*.
2. The ruler's _____ was a partner but not necessarily a wife or husband.

WORD PLAY
Look up the word that you did not use in the dictionary. Write that word in a sentence.

_____

Read the third paragraph on page 80. What is the difference between a consort in Cleopatra's time and a husband or wife today? _____

THE ANCIENT ROMAN WORLD

WHAT HAPPENED WHEN?

Fill in the events that happened in the dates below. Then copy them onto a timeline marked into five-year sections.

51 BCE _____

46 BCE _____

44 BCE _____

31 BCE _____

30 BCE _____

CRITICAL THINKING
COMPARE AND CONTRAST

The sentences below describe the actions of Caesar, Antony, and Cleopatra. The Venn diagram below uses three circles, one for each of these people. Now copy the phrases below in the correct circles. The phrases that apply to only one character go in that person's circle. The phrases that describe actions of two people go in the area where the two circles belonging to those two characters connect. Any actions of all three belong in the shaded area formed by all three circles. (You can also color the circles with light-colored markers or pencils and then use those colors to underline or circle the phrases which describe each character.)

committed suicide	defeated Ptolemy	hid in a carpet
was assassinated	lived in Rome	ruled Rome
was married	lived in Alexandria	went to Tarsus
had child by Caesar	lost to Octavian	dressed as servant
had children by Antony	lived with Cleopatra	

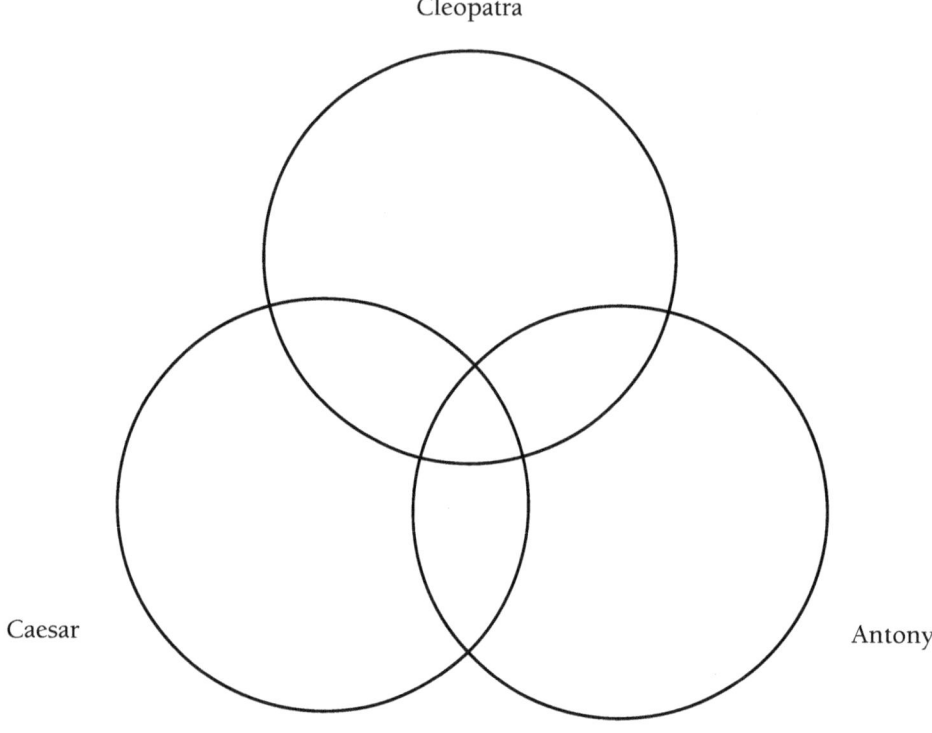

CHAPTER 13
THE EMPEROR'S NEW NAMES: THE REIGN OF AUGUSTUS

CHAPTER SUMMARY
The long rule of Augustus Caesar brought a period of peace to the Roman Empire.

ACCESS
Do you have a nickname? Does your family call you a different name from your friends? Augustus was known by several names throughout his life. Divide a page in your history journal into three columns. Label one column *Octavius* (his name as a boy). Label the second column *Octavian* (his name as a general). Label the third *Augustus* (his name as emperor). As you read the chapter, write at least three facts about Augustus under each of his names.

CAST OF CHARACTERS
Write two adjectives to describe each character. Then write why you chose them.

	Adjective	Why?
Augustus Caesar		
Julia		
Lepidus		
Tiberius		

WORD BANK
conspirator   confiscate   frontier   legitimate

Choose words from the Word Bank to complete the sentences. One word is not used at all.

1. In Roman times, a child whose parents were married was considered _____.
2. The word _____ came from the Latin word for "breathing."
3. _____ was based on the Latin term for "basket."

WORD PLAY
Look up the word that you did not use in the dictionary. Write that word in a sentence.

WITH A PARENT OR PARTNER

The prefix *con* means "with." In five minutes, write all the words you can think of that start with con. Ask a parent or partner to do the same. Then read your lists to each other. Look up in a dictionary any words either of you doesn't know.

WHAT HAPPENED WHEN?

Write the events that happened on these dates.

30 BCE _____
_____

27 BCE _____
_____

14 CE _____
_____

DO THE MATH

What year followed 1 BCE? _____

COMPREHENSION
SEQUENCE OF EVENTS

The sentences below describe events in the life of Augustus. Put them in order by writing numbers in the blanks next to each event. (Write "1" next to the earliest event, and so forth.)

_____ Octavian declared the *Pax Romana* and built the Altar of Peace.

_____ The Senate named Augustus a god.

_____ Octavian took the name "Augustus Caesar."

_____ Antony's wife and brother rebelled against Octavian.

_____ Caesar made Octavius his heir.

_____ Augustus named his stepson to succeed him.

_____ Antony took Caesar's money, property, and papers.

WORKING WITH PRIMARY SOURCES

Life of Augustus by Nicolas of Damascus (20 CE)

This excerpt describes Augustus—known then as Octavius—as a young boy:

> Octavius, at the age of about twelve years . . . showed great promise, already seeming to be treated with respect by . . . children of highest birth. Many . . . lads, men, and boys of his own age attended him whether he rode on horseback outside of the town or went to the house of his relations or any other person; for he exercised his mind with the finest practices and his body with . . . warlike pursuits. More quickly than his teachers he . . . applied his lesson to the facts in hand, so that for this reason also much praise [came] to him.

WRITE ABOUT IT

Imagine that you are a teacher writing a report card for 12-year-old Octavius. Begin like this: "Octavius is a fine student who is well liked by his classmates." Continue the report in your history journal.

CHAPTER 14
MISERY, MISTRUST, MADNESS, AND MURDER: THE SUCCESSORS OF AUGUSTUS

CHAPTER SUMMARY
The four emperors who followed Augustus ruled over a period of bloodshed, violence, and revolt.

ACCESS
COMPARE AND CONTRAST
The way governments are run depends a lot on the person at the top. They can change dramatically from one ruler's time to the next. Make a four-column chart. At the top of each column, write the name of one of the emperors in this chapter who ruled after Augustus. As you read, write down facts about what happened during each emperor's rule.

CAST OF CHARACTERS
Write several adjectives or character traits that describe each person below. Then write why you chose them.

                 Adjectives   Why?

Tiberius _____

Caligula _____

Claudius _____

Nero _____

Vespasian (vuh-SPAY-zhun) _____

Titus _____

Domitian (duh-MISH-un) _____

Claudius: Adjectives from the book that describe Claudius's disabilities did not describe his abilities. Look for adjectives in the third paragraph on page 98 to describe Claudius:

_____

WORD BANK
successor   palace   tyrant

Choose words from the Word Bank to complete the sentences. One word is not used at all.

1. A _____ does not always succeed in ruling well.
2. A _____ is not always the home of a successful ruler

WORD PLAY
Look up in a dictionary the word that you did not use. Write that word in a sentence.

_____

THE ANCIENT ROMAN WORLD

WHAT HAPPENED WHEN?

Write which emperor ruled in the time spans below

14–37 CE _____

37–41 CE _____

41–54 CE _____

54–68 CE _____

Why is this date important?

68 CE _____

Fill in all the dates in the right places on the chart you created under **Access**.

WORKING WITH PRIMARY SOURCES

Nero and the Great Fire

Roman History by Dio Cassius (225 CE)

> Nero sent out . . . men . . . and . . . had . . . fires kindled quietly. [Soon] . . . the screaming of children, women, men, and gray beards mingled together. . . . Many were suffocated or crushed. This . . . lasted several days and nights running. While the whole [city] was in this state of . . . calamity . . . Nero mounted upon the roof of the palace . . . and sang "The Taking of Troy."

Life of Nero by Suetonius (130 CE)

> [Displeased] at the . . . old buildings and the . . . crooked streets, [Nero] set fire to the city . . . openly. . . . For six days and seven nights destruction raged, while the people were driven for shelter to monuments and tombs. . . . Viewing the [fire] from the tower of Maecenas, and exulting . . . "with the beauty of the flames," he sang . . . "The Sack of Ilium."

Did You Know? In ancient Rome, Troy was called *Ilium*. To *sack* means "to conquer."

CRITICAL THINKING
FACT OR OPINION?

1. Read the last paragraph on page 99 and continue on to page 100. Is the sentence "Nero fiddled while Rome burned" a fact or an opinion?
   _____

   Now read the two versions, above, of the fire that destroyed Rome. Circle one fact and one opinion in each.

2. Which version of this story was written first? _____

3. How does Dio Cassius's version differ from Suetonius's account regarding how long the fire burned? _____

4. In what other ways do the two versions differ? How are they alike? _____
   _____

WRITE ABOUT IT

Imagine that you are a news reporter covering the fire. In your history journal, write a report of what you know or see—and also of rumors that you hear about the cause of the fire. Your headline is "ROME BURNS! THOUSANDS DIE! WHERE IS NERO?"

CHAPTER 15
CHILDHOOD AND MARRIAGE, MOTHERS AND MATRIARCHS: WOMEN AND CHILDREN

CHAPTER SUMMARY
Although women had fewer rights than men in Rome, they played an important role in Roman society.

ACCESS
Are girls and boys in the United States treated the same today? Take a minute to write down ways they are treated equally or unequally. In chapter 15, you will read about girls in ancient Rome. Copy the main idea map from page 8 of this workbook in your history journal. In the largest box write *Roman girls*. In each of the smaller boxes write one fact that you learn as you read the chapter.

CAST OF CHARACTERS
Write a few sentences about why each character is important.

Livia _____

_____

Julia Domna _____

_____

Julia Mammaea (mah-MAY-eye) _____

_____

DRAWING CONCLUSIONS
Read sentences five and six in the third paragraph on page 103.

1. What do you think were the names of the fathers of the women above?

_____

2. What conclusions could you draw about a Roman woman named *Julia Secunda*?

_____

WORD BANK
erased   identity   education   matriarch

Choose words from the Word Bank to complete the sentences. One word is not used at all.

1. A good _____ was available only to the children of wealthy families.
2. In Rome, mistakes were _____ from wax tablets.
3. Although a _____ helped Augustus, no Roman woman is called "the mother of her country."

WORD PLAY
Look up in a dictionary the word that you did not use. Write that word in a sentence.

_____

If a *matriarch* is a powerful woman, what is a *patriarch*? _____

(Hint: Think about the meaning of *paterfamilias* in Chapter 5.)

THE ANCIENT ROMAN WORLD

CRITICAL THINKING
MAKING INFERENCES

Roman girls and women had some rights, but they were also strictly controlled by men at all levels of society. Check off the phrases below that describe scenes that could really happen in ancient Rome.

_____ a peasant girl learns to read _____ a woman votes _____ a girl marries at 14
_____ a woman owns land _____ an infant girl is abandoned _____ a woman goes to a play
_____ a girl chooses her husband _____ a teenage girl goes to school _____ a girl works
_____ a woman earns money _____ a woman divorces a man _____ a woman lives alone
_____ a woman works with her husband _____ a girl plays sports _____ a woman reads
_____ an abused woman leaves her husband _____ a woman inherits her father's wealth

WORKING WITH PRIMARY SOURCES
A Poem by Sulpicia

The poems of Sulpicia are the only known poems written by a Roman woman.

> Birthday's here and I hate it—
> of all the days to be spent in gloom
> out in the dreary country
> without Cerinthus.
> What is sweeter than the city?
> Is a house in the country
> on the banks of that frigid stream in Arretine country,
> any place for a girl?
> Now Uncle Masella do take a rest—
> you've always looked after me too well.
> There are times, you know, when travel's
> a bad idea.

MAKING INFERENCES

1. What kind of mood do you think Sulpicia was in when she wrote the poem? Why?
   _____

2. Cerinthus is probably Sulpicia's _____ brother _____ father _____ boyfriend

3. Why does Sulpicia write "There are times, you know, when travel's a bad idea"?
   _____

4. Read the second paragraph on page 104. How do you know that Sulpicia was an aristocrat?
   _____

WRITE ABOUT IT

Reread the third paragraph on page 105. Then write a letter in your history journal, choosing one of the following two scenarios:

1. You are Sulpicia, writing a letter to Cerinthus. Your family has just had a Roman writer to dinner, someone who has the same opinions as Juvenal. In your letter, describe to Cerinthus how this guest's opinions about women and poetry made you feel. Do you agree with him? What would he say about the fact that you knew how to write? Did his comments make you angry?

2. You are Cerinthus, writing a letter to Sulpicia. You have just been walking in the Roman Forum with someone very much like Juvenal. In your letter, describe to Sulpicia your conversation with this man. What opinions did he share about women and literature? Did you agree with him? How would you explain your conversation to Sulpicia?

CHAPTER 16: A CITY TELLS ITS TALE: POMPEII AND THE ROMAN HOUSE

CHAPTER SUMMARY

The eruption of Mount Vesuvius destroyed two Roman cities, but the disaster preserved Roman life for archaeologists to study thousands of years later.

ACCESS

What kind of natural disaster is the biggest problem in your area? Some parts of the United States are hit by tornadoes or hurricanes. Some are struck by blizzards. The eruption of the volcano Mount Vesuvius was one of the greatest natural disasters in the ancient world. For Pliny the Elder, the day of the disaster began like any other. In your history journal, make a timeline of Pliny's day. Begin at 7 a.m. and mark off in hour sections until 4 p.m. Fill in the timeline with activities Pliny did on August 24 as you read the chapter.

CAST OF CHARACTERS

Write a few sentences about why the following people were important.

Pliny (PLIH-nee) the Elder _____

_____

Pliny the Younger _____

_____

WORD BANK

plumbing   volcano   archeologists

Choose words from the Word Bank to complete the sentences. One word is not used at all.

The pathways from the interior of a _____ that bring lava to the surface are like the _____ lines that carry waste water away from homes.

WORD PLAY

Look up in a dictionary the word that you did not use. Write that word in a sentence.

_____

GROUP TOGETHER

The suffix *-ology* means "the study of." Gather in a small group and think of all the words you can that end with *-ology*. Write them down. Then look up what they mean. Read lists aloud to each other. Guess meanings of words you don't know, then check them in a dictionary.

THE ANCIENT ROMAN WORLD

MAKING INFERENCES

In the book, read the information about plumbing and its relation to lead. Today, scientists know that lead causes mental illness and that water was carried into the homes of wealthy Romans in lead-lined pipes. Wealthy Romans often mixed wine with water. Why might some historians use this information to explain the actions of emperors such as Caligula? (Chapter 14, page 97)

WHAT HAPPENED WHEN?

Why is this date important?

August 24, 79 CE _____

WORKING WITH PRIMARY SOURCES

Natural History: Luxury in the Use of Rings, by Pliny the Elder

> It was the custom at first to wear rings on a single finger only—the one next to the little finger. Later it became usual to put rings on the finger next to the thumb . . . and more recently still it has been the fashion to wear them upon the little finger too . . . smaller rings even being [worn on] smaller joints of the fingers. Some people thrust several rings upon the little finger alone. . . [and] . . . make a parade of their rings. . . . Others . . . [hide] poisons beneath their ring stones, and . . . wear them as instruments of death. . . . Happy the times . . . when no [ring] was ever [worn]!

COMPREHENSION

Read the last paragraph on page 112 and answer the following questions.

1. What two things did the woman and three servants have "in their hands"? _____
2. According to Pliny, how did the Roman custom of wearing rings change? _____
   _____

3. When Pliny says people "make a parade of their rings," he means they
   a. _____ show off.
   b. _____ march with soldiers.
   c. _____ line up their rings.

4. How do you think Pliny feels about the way Roman ring wearing has changed?
   _____
   _____

WRITE ABOUT IT

Imagine that you are a 19th-century archaeologist working in Pompeii. You have injected plaster into a space where one of the volcano's victims died. In your history journal, describe or draw a design of the rings that person was wearing at the time of the disaster.

CHAPTER 17
ALL THE EMPEROR'S MEN: TRAJAN AND THE ARMY

CHAPTER SUMMARY
The Roman army played a significant military and economic role in the expansion of the Roman Empire.

ACCESS
Do you have a friend or family member who is in the armed forces? What is life like for him or her? Life in the Roman army was often difficult and dangerous. In your history journal, copy the K-W-L chart from page 8 of this book. In the first column, write everything you already *know* about the life of a Roman soldier (if you don't know anything, that's okay). In the middle column, write down what you *want to know*. After you read the chapter, write everything that you have learned about Roman military life in the third column.

CAST OF CHARACTERS
Write a few sentences about why each character was important.

Nerva (NERV-uh) _____
_____

Trajan (TRAY-jun) _____
_____

What relation was Trajan to Nerva? _____

WORD BANK
legacy

Find the sentence in which the word *legacy* appears. Rewrite the sentence using the definition of the word.
_____
_____

Write a few sentences that explain the "legacy" of Trajan's rule.
_____
_____
_____

THE ANCIENT ROMAN WORLD **43**

CRITICAL THINKING
CAUSE AND EFFECT

Each "cause" in the left column tells what helped the Roman Empire expand. Match the "causes" with the "effects" in the right-hand column. (There is one extra effect.)

CAUSE	EFFECT
1. Trajan was not raised in Rome,	a. SO he treated senators as equals.
2. Centurions were the backbone of the army,	b. SO he was not drawn in to political plots and schemes
3. Attacking Roman soldiers formed a "testudo,"	c. SO they could protect their heads and sides.
4. Soldiers built roads in peacetime,	d. SO they chose to return to the fields for farm work.
5. Soldiers were stationed in distant provinces,	e. SO their salaries helped support local economies.
6. As emperor, Trajan wanted to guide, not control,	f. SO travel to distant regions of the empire was easier.
	g. SO they were paid much more than foot soldiers.

WORKING WITH PRIMARY SOURCES

Lucius Seneca (written about 63 CE)

Read the sidebar on page 117 about the Roman baths. Write one sentence giving your opinion about the baths. _____

_____

Now read this essay by the famous Roman playwright Lucius Seneca.

> I live over a bathing establishment. Picture . . . the assortment of voices . . . which is enough to sicken one. . . . When the stronger fellows are exercising. . . . working hard or pretending to be working hard, I hear their groans . . . their hissing and jarring breathing. Add to this the . . . fellow who always likes to hear his own voice in the bath, and those who jump into the pool with a mighty splash as they strike the water. Imagine the hair plucker keeping up a constant chatter . . . never silent except when he is plucking armpits and making the customer yell instead of yelling himself.

1. What is Seneca's opinion of living over a bathhouse?
2. From the essay, what activities can you tell take place at a bath house?
3. What is the job of the hair plucker?
    a. _____ To give haircuts
    b. _____ To remove body hair
4. How is Seneca's essay about the bath different from the sidebar on page 117?

WRITE ABOUT IT

Imagine that you are visiting Rome from the country. You go to a bathhouse. In your journal, write a letter to your family describing what you see. Start with: "Dear mother and father, I am writing to you after returning from the baths. I met many interesting people there, and I was amazed at how pleasant and beautiful the building was." Continue with at least four more sentences. Give an opinion about the baths.

CHAPTER 18
PLEASING THE ROWDY ROMANS: GLADIATORS AND CIRCUSES

CHAPTER SUMMARY
Popular entertainment for Romans featured competitions, fights, and cruelty.

ACCESS
Think of your two favorite activities, like playing sports or video games. Romans had favorites, too. Draw a three-circle Venn diagram in your history journal. Label one circle with one of your favorite pastimes. Label the second with another favorite. Label the third *Gladiators and Circuses*. Write as many thoughts as you can about all three topics. Write any thoughts that are similar to two circles in the shaded area where two circles connect. Any thoughts that connect all three circles belong in the shaded area formed by all three circles.

CAST OF CHARACTERS
Write a few sentences about why each character was important.

Plautus _____

Diocles _____

How would you know by looking at the names above that Plautus and Diocles were men?
_____

WORD BANK
sword   arena   Saturnalia   shield   gladiators   chariot   trident   net   mercy   *ludi*

Complete the paragraph below by writing the words from the Word Bank in the blanks.

Although he was a loyal Roman, the writer Seneca did not enjoy attending the _____. While he enjoyed celebrating at festivals such as _____, he preferred to avoid the violence that was on display at the open _____. Sometimes he bet on a _____ race, but he had no stomach for the bloody fights between _____. The sight of a fighter slashing with a _____ and protecting himself with a _____ drove fans wild. Others preferred a cat-quick fighter who threw a _____ over their opponents and pierced them with a three-forked _____. For Seneca, the bloodthirsty cries of the crowd and their refusal to show any _____ represented the worst of Roman society.

WORD PLAY
Read the sidebar about the word *gladiator* on page 125. Then look up a photo of the flower called *gladiolus*. How do you think the flower got its name? (Hint: Notice its shape.)

What day of the week is named after the god who is honored in the biggest Roman festival?
_____

THE ANCIENT ROMAN WORLD

WORKING WITH PRIMARY SOURCES

Lucius Seneca

Read Seneca's letter on page 127. What does he mean by "harmful to one's character"?

_____

_____

Now read the letter from Seneca to his friend Lucilius.

Epistle 7: The Gladiatorial Games

    I [re]turned in to the games one mid-day hoping for a little wit and humor there. I was bitterly disappointed. It was really mere butchery. The morning's show was merciful compared to it. Then men were thrown to lions and to bears: but at midday to the audience. There was no escape for them. The gladiator was [forced to fight] until he could be [killed.]

MAKING INFERENCES

1. What did Seneca see in the morning that he considered "merciful"?

_____

2. A butcher cuts up pieces of meat. What made the mid-day games "butchery" in Seneca's view?

_____

_____

3. What is Seneca's opinion of the crowds who watch the games?

    a. _____ He admires them.

    b. _____ He despises them.

    c. _____ He ignores them.

WRITE ABOUT IT

Imagine that you can go back to Roman times and attend a gladiatorial game. In your history journal, write a description of what you see. Compare your observations with any modern-day sport such as football, basketball, or soccer. Imagine talking with a Roman spectator. How would you describe the modern-day sport so that an ancient Roman person could imagine it? What comparisons could you make to the gladiatorial games?

You may want to put your comparisons in the form of a Venn diagram (see page 9). Write similarities between the modern sport and the gladiatorial game in the area where the two circles overlap. Write any differences in the parts of the circles that do not overlap.

GROUP TOGETHER

Wouldn't it be interesting to know what other students think about Roman entertainment? How was it similar to or different from entertainment today? Get a few friends together and ask your teacher to help you organize a discussion group at school. Have one person take notes and another person present the group's ideas to the class.

CHAPTER 19
HOW TO GET RICH IN ROME: BUSINESS AND TRADE

CHAPTER SUMMARY
As the Roman Empire expanded, trade routes were established and a merchant class of Romans arose.

ACCESS
What is your favorite store? Where do the things you like to buy at the store come from? In Roman times, food, cloth, and other products were shipped over long distances to be bought and sold. In your history journal, copy the K-W-L graphic organizer on page 8 of this study guide into your history journal. In the first column, write down anything you might know about business and trade in Rome (if you don't know anything, that's okay). In the second column, list several questions you have about these topics. As you read the chapter, make notes in the third column that answer your questions in the second column.

CAST OF CHARACTERS
Write a few words about why the following character was important.

Eumachia (u-MAH-chee-uh) _____

WORD BANK
import   patron   monsoon

Choose words from the Word Bank to complete the sentence. One word is not used.

1. A _____ often provided money to help merchants pay for goods they wanted to _____.

WORD PLAY
Look up the word that you did not use in the dictionary. Write that word in a sentence.

_____

WITH A PARENT OR PARTNER
The words *import* and *important* share the same Latin root *importare*, which means "to bring in." What does *port* mean? With a friend or parent, see how many other words you can think of that have *port* in them. List as many as you can think of in one minute. Read lists aloud to each other. Look up any words you don't know.

_____

CRITICAL THINKING
The prefix *ex* means "from." The prefix *im* means "into." *Exports* are goods sent out of a country. To *export* something means to send it out of a country. *Imports* are goods brought into a country. To *import* something means to receive it into a country. The items in the box are mentioned in the chapter. Complete the sentences below by writing *export* or *import* in the blanks.

iron	grain	silk	amber	glass	pepper	ivory	paper
	wine	marble	wool	olives			

THE ANCIENT ROMAN WORLD

1. A Roman merchant might _____ _____ to be used in clothing and yarn
2. A Roman jeweler might _____ _____ to be used in rings and bracelets.
3. A wealthy Roman might _____ _____ for sculptures and _____ for windows.
4. A wealthy Roman might _____ _____ from China to make the finest clothes.
5. A Roman merchant might _____ _____ that could be pressed into oil.
6. A Roman writer might _____ _____ to use for his work.
7. A Roman merchant might _____ _____ to add flavor to his food.
8. A Roman merchant might _____ _____ to be ground into flour for bread.

ALL OVER THE MAP
INTERACTION
Study the map of Roman trade in 200 CE. For background, read from the last paragraph on page 131 through page 132. Then use the mileage scale to answer the following questions. (Give distances in both miles and kilometers. To calculate kilometers, use the mileage scale or multiply the miles by 1.61.)

1. How long was the silk route from China to the eastern shore of the Mediterranean Sea?
2. How long was the monsoon route from Egypt to the southern tip of India?
3. How long was the amber route?
4. Which two products had the farthest to go to reach Rome?
5. Which two products were closest to Rome?

REGIONS
1. Use shading and patterns to show the territories of the Roman, Persian, and Chinese empires.
2. Complete the legend on the map to identify each of your patterns.

WRITE ABOUT IT
Imagine that you are a Roman citizen watching ships enter and leave the harbor at Naples. Write a diary entry in your history journal about seeing ivory or glass for the first time. Describe the item without using its name.

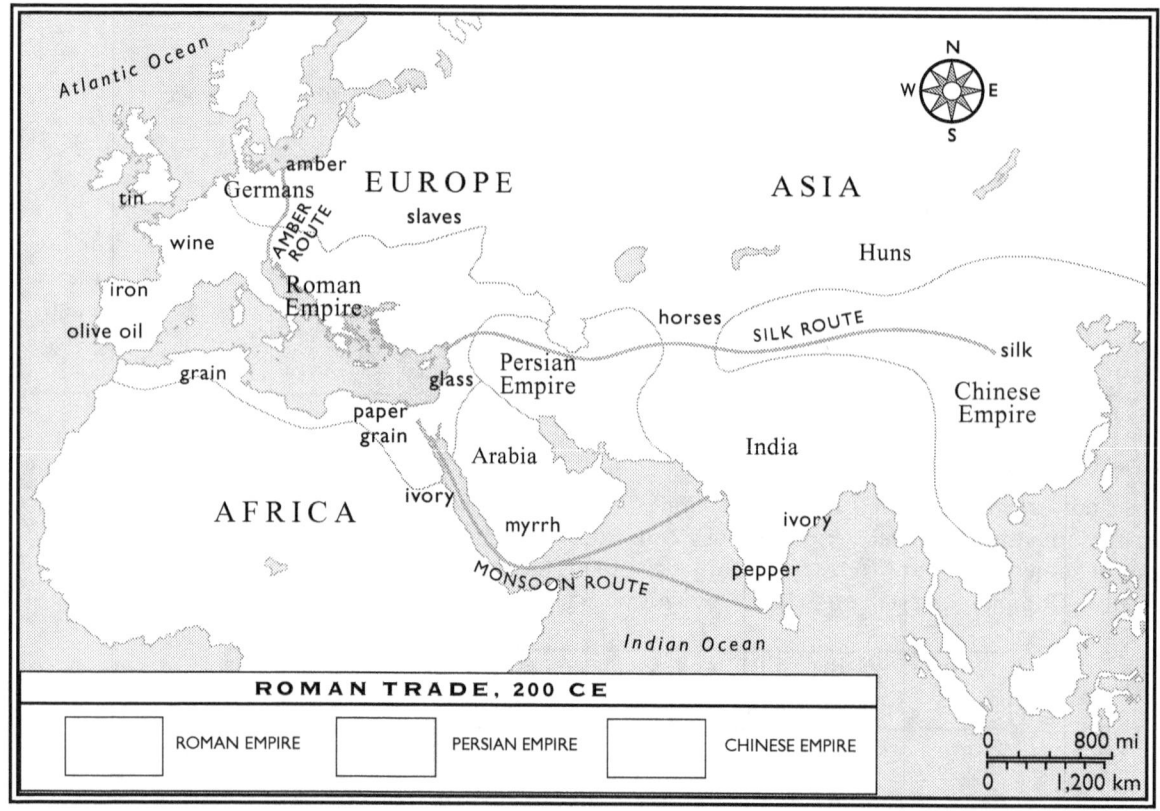

ROMAN TRADE, 200 CE

□ ROMAN EMPIRE   □ PERSIAN EMPIRE   □ CHINESE EMPIRE

CHAPTER 20
THE RESTLESS BUILDER: THE EMPEROR HADRIAN

CHAPTER SUMMARY
Hadrian was a practical leader who believed in strong defenses, and he was an artist who admired other cultures.

ACCESS
Who is the most talented adult you know? What things can that person do well? Hadrian, too, was a person who had many interests and many different skills. In your history journal, copy the main idea graphic organizer from page 8 of this study guide. In the largest box write *Hadrian*. In each of the smaller boxes write one fact that you learn as you read the chapter.

CAST OF CHARACTERS
Explain in two or more sentences why the following character was important.

Hadrian (HAY-dree-un)

_____

_____

_____

WORD BANK
pagan

Look up the definition of *pagan* in a dictionary. Write the word in a sentence.

_____

WHAT HAPPENED WHEN?
MAKING COMPARISONS
Trajan and Hadrian ruled from 98 CE to 138 CE. Write two sentences comparing the period of their rules with the period from 14 CE to 68 CE when Tiberius, Caligula, Claudius, and Nero ruled (review chapters 14 and 17).

_____

_____

BUILDING A TIMELINE
In your history journal, copy the timeline graphic organizer from page 9. Write *Major events in the rules of Trajan and Hadrian* as your timeline title. On your dateline, begin with 100 CE and end with 150 CE. Mark off 10-year segments. Then list all the major events that took place in Rome during this period.

THE ANCIENT ROMAN WORLD

CRITICAL THINKING
DRAWING CONCLUSIONS

As an emperor, Hadrian was a practical ruler. But he was also an artistic person. Write the letter "L" next to the sentences below that describe Hadrian as a leader. Write "A" next to those sentences that describe him as an artist. Write "B" next to those sentences that describe him as both leader and artist.

1. _____ Greek literature, art, and music especially fascinated him.
2. _____ He was a painter and sculptor who worshiped beauty both in art and nature.
3. _____ Hadrian . . . traveled . . . to make sure the army . . . was ready for battle.
4. _____ He enjoyed talking to common men and even went to the public baths.
5. _____ Hadrian was friendly with soldiers, but he also knew that strict discipline was important.
6. _____ Hadrian wanted to avoid unnecessary wars.
7. _____ Each building Hadrian designed was a copy of a place he had admired in his travels.

WORKING WITH PRIMARY SOURCES

Aelius Spartianus (125 CE)

> [Hadrian] loved poetry. . . . He understood . . . arithmetic, geometry, and painting. He danced and sang extremely well. . . . He . . . was a master of the military art . . . [and] devoted . . . to the exercises of gladiators. Now severe, now merry . . . now cruel, now merciful, this Emperor seemed never the same. He enriched his friends . . . but . . . growing suspicious of some put them to death. . . .

1. Circle words that show how Hadrian could be "merry" and "merciful."
2. Circle words that show how he could be "cruel" and "severe."
3. What do you think Aelius means when he says Hadrian was a "master of the military art"?
   a. He painted exciting battles.
   b. He was a skilled leader in battle.
   c. He gave orders.

WRITE ABOUT IT

Imagine you are a reporter in ancient Rome. Your task is to write a profile of Hadrian at the end of his life at the beautiful villa he designed near Rome. Write down the questions you would ask him. Then imagine his answers and write the profile based on your interview.

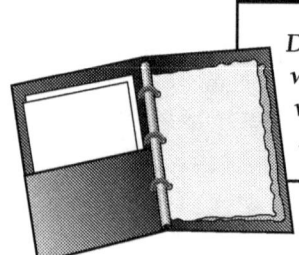

HISTORY JOURNAL

Don't forget to share your history journal with your classmates, and ask if you can see what their journals look like. You might be surprised—and get some new ideas.

CHAPTER 21
MAGIC AND THE CULTS OF THE NEAR EAST: NEW RELIGIOUS IDEAS

CHAPTER SUMMARY
Romans were superstitious and worshipped gods from other regions of the empire.

ACCESS
What magic tricks have you seen people perform? How do you think the trick was done? In Rome, magic and cults were part of daily life. In your history journal, copy the main idea map graphic organizer from page 9 of this workbook. In the largest box, write *Magic and Cults*. In each of the smaller boxes, write one fact that you learn as you read the chapter. When you finish the chapter, return to the main idea map and label each box *magic* or *cults* based on what you have learned.

CAST OF CHARACTERS
Write why each character was important.

Cybele _____

Isis _____

Mithras _____

DRAWING CONCLUSIONS
In the myth of Cybele, her loved one dies from illness. In the myth of Isis, her husband is murdered. Both come back to life. Mithra, the sun god, "died" at night and "came to life" at dawn. Write two sentences explaining why you think myths about death and rebirth became popular among average Romans.

_____

_____

WORD BANK
supernatural   astrology   superstitious   fertility

Choose words from the Word Bank to complete the sentences. Two words are not used at all.

1. A Roman who was _____ believed in good luck charms.
2. A Roman who believed in a _____ goddess hoped to have healthy children.

WORD PLAY
Look up in a dictionary the two words that you did not use. Write one sentence that includes both words.

_____

THE ANCIENT ROMAN WORLD

WITH A PARENT OR PARTNER

In Latin, *super* means "over" or "above." In one minute, list in your journal as many words as you can think of that start with *super*. For extra fun, challenge a parent or partner to make a list, too. Then compare lists by reading aloud. Look up any unfamiliar words in a dictionary.

CRITICAL THINKING

Romans were superstitious people who worshipped gods of many religions. Write "S" next to the words from the chapter below that refer to superstition. Write "R" next to the words that refer to religion.

_____ witches _____ evil eye _____ sacrifice _____ woodland spirits

_____ rebirth _____ omens _____ spiders _____ ringing ears

_____ spells _____ charms _____ black meteorite _____ life after death

_____ planets and stars _____ sun _____ emperor _____ blossoming flowers

_____ fertility

WORKING WITH PRIMARY SOURCES

Satyricon by Petronius (66 CE)

Read the second paragraph on page 140. Write a definition of astrology based on what you read.

Astrology is _____

Now read this excerpt from the *Satyricon*. "Trimalchio" is the host of a large banquet:

> Trimalchio interrupted . . . "Look now, these . . . heavens . . . there are twelve gods living [there]. First [is] the Ram . . . Most scholars are born under this sign, and most muttonheads as well. Then the . . . heavens turn into the . . . Bull. So bullheaded folk are born then. . . . I was born under the Crab, so I have a lot of legs to stand on and a lot of property on land and sea, because the Crab takes both in his stride. Under Leo are born . . . bossy people. Under Scorpio poisoners and murderers. . . . Under the fishes . . . people who spout in public.

1. Do you think Trimalchio believes in astrology or that he is making fun of it? Explain in your journal.
2. What do you think Trimalchio means by the term "muttonhead"?
3. What is another word for people who are "bullheaded"?
   a. _____ strong
   b. _____ stubborn
   c. _____ loud
   d. _____ cowardly
4. What might Trimalchio mean when he says he has "a lot of legs to stand on"?
   a. _____ more than two legs
   b. _____ many strong opinions
   c. _____ many friends
   d. _____ many places where he is welcome
   e. _____ a love of seafood

WRITE ABOUT IT

Imagine that you were born under the sign of Leo, and you are a guest at the banquet. When Trimalchio finishes his speech, it is your turn to talk. "Dear Trimalchio," you say, "I am insulted that you consider me a bossy person. Instead, I consider myself . . ." (Continue with two to three sentences. Write in your journal.)

CHAPTER 22
TAXES AND TACTICS IN THE PROVINCES: ADMINISTERING THE EMPIRE

CHAPTER SUMMARY
The economy of the Roman Empire was based on a well-organized system of census and taxation under the control of local administrators.

ACCESS
How do you get the money you spend? Do you have a job or get an allowance? How do you manage the money you earn? The way a country makes and manages its money is called its *economy*. To organize information about the Roman economy, use the outline graphic organizer on page 8 of this book. As you read the chapter, identify two or more main ideas that relate to Rome's economy (for example, "taxation" and "census"). Write these down on the lines labeled *Main Idea*. Add any details about each main idea in the lines below.

CAST OF CHARACTERS
Write a few words about why the following character was important.

Agricola (uh-GRI-cuh-luh) _____

WORD BANK
customs   enemy   ocher   forum

Choose words from the Word Bank to complete the sentences. Two words are not used at all.

1. Someone who was not an *amicus* was an _____.
2. Women who used _____ colored their lips either yellow or red.

WORD PLAY
Look up in a dictionary the two words that you did not use. Write one sentence that includes both words.

_____

The Latin root word *amicus* is used to make the English word "amicable," which means "friendly." Do you know words for "friend" in other languages based on Latin, such as Spanish, Italian, French, or Portuguese? Write them here.

_____

THE ANCIENT ROMAN WORLD   53

ALL OVER THE MAP

Where did the following peoples live in the Roman Empire?

1. Britons _____
2. Celts _____
3. Palestinians _____
4. Why do you think the Roman census required people to return to their hometowns for a census?
_____

COMPREHENSION
SEQUENCE OF EVENTS

The sentences below explain how the Roman Empire grew and changed over 500 years. Use numbers to put the events in their proper order to explain the pattern of movement and growth. You may want to use the sequence of events chart on page 9.

_____ Taxes were assessed and collected by local officials.

_____ Provincial culture was brought back to Rome with returning officials and soldiers.

_____ Roman culture was established.

_____ Census was taken among newly conquered provincials.

_____ Roman armies conquered a province.

_____ Governors and tax collectors were sent from Rome.

_____ Languages and religion of Rome and provinces mixed.

_____ Soldiers established control and built fortifications in an area.

WORKING WITH PRIMARY SOURCES

Calcagus's Speech, from *The Histories* by Tacitus

Read the first portion of Calcagus's speech to his troops on page 144. Would you say that Calcagus is calling the Romans strong or weak?
_____

Why? _____
_____

Now read the final portion of the speech.

> The reputation of the Roman army is built . . . on the [weakness] of its enemies. . . . All that can lead men to victory is on our side. The [Romans] have no wives to fire their courage, no parents . . . to taunt them if they run away. . . . See them . . . scared and bewildered, staring blankly at the unfamiliar sky, sea and forests. . . . The gods have given them . . . into our hands. Never fear the outward show that means nothing. . . .

1. How is the final portion of the speech different from the first part on page 144? Write your answer in your history journal.
2. What do you think Calcagus means when he says "never fear the outward show"? Explain your answer in you history journal.

WRITE ABOUT IT

Read the words of Ceralis after the Romans conquer Britain on page 144. Now imagine the speech he might have given to his troops before they battled Calcagus's troops. Begin with these words: "Mighty soldiers! I know you are far from home, but you must remember: You are the great Roman army. Your victories have been many!" Add three to four sentences to inspire the Romans to fight. Write in your history journal.

CHAPTER 23
ONE GOD OR MANY? THE JEWS OF THE ROMAN EMPIRE

CHAPTER SUMMARY
The Jews, the only ancient people to worship a single god, struggled for religious freedom against the Roman emperors.

ACCESS
How would a timeline of your life be different from a timeline of a parent or other adult? Make a timeline from the years shown in the sidebar on page 152. Now place an X near the date for the founding of Rome. (If you can't remember the date, go back to Chapter 1.) What does your timeline show about the difference between the history of the Jewish people and the history of the Roman Empire?

CAST OF CHARACTERS
Write why each character was important.

Titus _____

David _____

Solomon _____

Antiochus IV _____

Judas Maccabeus _____

WORD BANK
Sabbath   scripture   kosher   Yahweh   client

Choose words from the Word Bank to complete the sentences. Two words are not used at all.

1. A country that is a _____ of another nation is protected by that nation.
2. A food must be prepared according to strict religious law to be _____.
3. For the Jews, _____ was the one true God.

WORD PLAY
Look up the two words that you did not use in the dictionary. Write one sentence that includes both words.

_____

WITH A PARENT OR PARTNER
The word "scripture" comes from the Latin word *scriptura*, meaning "the product of writing." In your journal, list as many words as you can think of in one minute that contain the core word *script*. For extra fun, ask a parent or family member or partner to make a list too. Then compare lists by reading aloud. Look up any new words in a dictionary.

CRITICAL THINKING
CAUSE AND EFFECT

Each cause listed in the left-hand column tells what happened between the Jews and the Romans as the Roman Empire expanded. Draw a line between each cause and its effect, shown in the right-hand column, to make sentences that tell what followed. You may also want to use the cause and effect chart on page 9.

CAUSE	EFFECT
1. Judas Maccabeus sent ambassadors to Rome,	a. AND he put the hated Herod on the throne.
2. Pompey conquered Judea,	b. AND he tried to force Greek and Roman culture on them.
3. Mark Antony made Judea a client kingdom,	c. AND traditional sacrifices were no longer allowed.
4. Herod didn't sympathize with Jewish beliefs,	d. AND Rome made the new Jewish state an ally.
5. After Masada, priests no longer led the Jewish people,	e. AND Jews were scattered across the Roman Empire.
6. Hadrian defeated Simon Bar Kochbar in 135 CE,	f. AND he dishonored all that was sacred to the Jews.

WORKING WITH PRIMARY SOURCES

Histories, by Tacitus (110 CE)

Read Tacitus's description of Jewish beliefs.

> The Jews have . . . mental conceptions of [God] as one . . .
>
> They believe [God] to be supreme and eternal . . .
>
> They call those [wicked] who [make images] . . . of God in human shape out of perishable materials. They . . . do not allow images (of God) to stand . . . in . . . their temples. Flattery is not paid to . . . to our Emperors. . . . The Jewish religion is tasteless and [low].

1. Circle the words that give Tacitus's opinion about the Jewish religion.
2. Think about the date when this was written. What has happened to the Jewish people by that time? Explain, using complete sentences, in your journal.
3. How do you think Tacitus feels about the fact that "Flattery is not paid to our Emperors"? Explain your answer in your journal.

WRITE ABOUT IT

Imagine you are a Jewish historian. How would you describe the Roman religion to your people? Write a short essay that describes the major differences between Judaism and the Roman beliefs. You may want to organize your ideas first. Use the outline graphic organizer on page 8 of this book to list two or more main ideas. Fill in details in the lines under each main idea.

GROUP TOGETHER

Wouldn't it be interesting to know what other students think about the conflicts between the Jews and the Romans? Get a few friends together and ask your teacher to help you organize a discussion group at school. Have one person take notes and another person present the group's ideas to the class.

CHAPTER 24
FROM JESUS TO CONSTANTINE: THE RISE OF CHRISTIANITY

CHAPTER SUMMARY
Over the course of three centuries, the spread of Christianity created enormous change in the Roman Empire.

ACCESS
According to studies, more than 2 billion people around the world are Christians. In the United States, more than 75 percent of Americans who belong to a religion are Christians. Yet in the early days of Christianity, those who followed its teachings faced torture and death. In your history journal, copy the K-W-L graphic organizer from page 8 of this book. In the *Know* column, write the two facts above. In the *What I Want to Know* columns, write three questions that you have. After reading the chapter, complete the *What I Learned* columns with facts about Christianity that help to explain its rise.

CAST OF CHARACTERS
Copy the Cast of Characters into your history journal. Write two adjectives that describe each character below. Then explain why you chose these words.

	Adjectives	Why you chose them
Jesus Christ	_____	_____
Herod	_____	_____
Pontius Pilate	_____	_____
Paul	_____	_____
Constantine	_____	_____

Tarsus, the city where Paul was born, was the center of the cult of Mithras, the sun god. (See chapter 21.) The main festival of the cult was held on December 25. What well-known modern holiday falls on the same day? _____

WORD BANK
Beatitudes   disciples   gospel   Messiah   persecuted   martyr

Complete the paragraph that follows with words from the Word Bank. One word is not used.

Jesus of Nazareth was known as the _____, or savior. His story began in the small village of Bethlehem. According to the _____, or book, of Matthew, by the time Jesus became a young man, he was speaking to large crowds. The crowds gathered around Jesus and his followers, or _____. Among the well-known words of Jesus are sayings called the _____. These begin with the word "blessed." Jesus preached ideas different from the establishment. This led to his being crucified. For centuries afterward, those who believed his ideas, called *Christians*, were _____.

THE ANCIENT ROMAN WORLD

WORD PLAY

Look up in a dictionary the word that you did not use. Write a sentence using the word. Include a character from the Cast of Characters.

_____

The term *Beatitudes* comes from the Latin word *beatificus*, which means "making happy." How did the Beatitudes make average people happy?

_____

COMPREHENSION
SEQUENCE OF EVENTS

The pairs of words below describe the life of Jesus and the rise of Christianity. Write *before* or *after* in the blank to correctly complete each sentence. Go back to the book as often as you need to.

1. Hebrew prophets wrote about a Messiah _____ Jesus was born.
2. Herod ordered the slaughter of all newborn babies in Bethlehem _____ Jesus was born.
3. Mary and Joseph returned from Egypt _____ Herod died.
4. Saul changed his name to Paul _____ he regained his sight.
5. Paul was put to death _____ a fire destroyed Rome.
6. Many Christians were tortured _____ the fire that destroyed Rome.
7. Constantine had a vision of a cross _____ an important battle.
8. Christianity spread quickly _____ Constantine decided to worship Christ.
9. A "New Rome" was built in Asia Minor _____ Constantine died.

WORKING WITH PRIMARY SOURCES

"Nero's Persecution of the Christians," by Tacitus

Read the first sentence in the fourth paragraph on page 159. Then read the description below, which is the first time Christians are mentioned in Roman history.

> Nero falsely accused and executed . . . those people called Christians. . . . The originator of the name, Christ, was executed as a criminal . . . [but] this destructive superstition erupted again, not only through Judea, which was the origin of this evil, but also through the city of Rome . . . Therefore, [Christians] were seized . . . [and] nailed to crosses.

IDENTIFYING POINT OF VIEW

Look closely at the words Tacitus uses to describe the Christians. Then answer the questions.

1. Would Tacitus agree or disagree with these words from page 159 about Nero: "he invented charges against the Christians"? _____

   Circle the words that support your answer.

2. What two words does Tacitus use to describe Christianity that indicate how he feels about it?
   _____ _____

WRITE ABOUT IT

Imagine that you are a Roman who has begun to believe that the Christians are being treated cruelly and unfairly. Write a diary entry in your history journal that begins: "Perhaps the Christians set the fire, but not all could be guilty of the crime." Continue with at least three more sentences. Express your feelings after seeing how Nero has punished the Christians.

CHAPTER 25

ROME'S POWER SLIPS AWAY: THE BARBARIANS

CHAPTER SUMMARY

The movement of barbarian tribes across the Rhine and Danube Rivers eventually led to the collapse of the Roman Empire.

ACCESS

BUILDING BACKGROUND

Barbarian tribes came from all over the Mediterranean region to attack Rome, often covering large distances. Study the map on page 165. In your history journal, make a chart with three columns. Label one column *Huns*, label the second column *Goths* and label the last column *Vandals*. Using the mileage scale, calculate and record in your chart how far the different groups traveled throughout the empire. Take notes as you read the chapter, and note in your chart what barriers the different tribes faced on their journeys. Note physical barriers such as rivers, mountains, and large bodies of water.

CAST OF CHARACTERS

Write why each character was important.

Varus (VAIR-us) _____

Arminius (ar-MIN-ee-us) _____

Marcus Aurelius (aw-RILL-ee-us) _____

Attila (AH-tull-uh) _____

WORD BANK

barbarian

Read the sidebar on page 164. Review the definition of the word "pagan" from chapter 20. In your journal, write two sentences that explain the difference between a pagan and a barbarian.

Did You Know? The modern nation of Hungary was the area in which the Huns settled when they came from Central Asia.

WORD PLAY

The "Sack of Rome" occurred in 410 CE, when the Goths captured the city. What is the meaning of the term *sack* in American football? (Hint: Try using a thesaurus.)

_____

THE ANCIENT ROMAN WORLD

CRITICAL THINKING
DRAWING CONCLUSIONS
Each of the sentences in *italics* below is taken from the chapter. Put a check mark in front of the conclusions that can be drawn from reading the sentence.

1. *As the Romans expanded their borders into Gaul, Spain, Germany, and Britain, they met peoples who knew nothing of Greek or Roman culture.*
   a. The peoples the Romans met did not speak Latin.
   b. The peoples the Romans met had armies more powerful than Rome's armies.
   c. The peoples the Romans met became subjects of the empire.

2. *The Romans assumed that these unfamiliar peoples were cruel and had no self-control.*
   a. The Romans were kind and caring rulers.
   b. The Romans believed they were superior to the unfamiliar peoples.
   c. The Romans were frightened by the unfamiliar peoples.

3. *The Goths ransacked the city, destroying or stealing at will, an event called the "Sack of Rome."*
   a. Innocent people died during the Sack of Rome.
   b. The Goths were the first barbarians ever to defeat the Roman army.
   c. There was no way to stop the Goths once they were inside the city.

4. *The idea of Roma Aeterna—Eternal Rome—had long been proclaimed by its rulers and celebrated by its writers.*
   a. Romans believed their city would never be conquered.
   b. Romans believed they would live forever.
   c. Romans always believed what their rulers and writers told them.

WORKING WITH PRIMARY SOURCES
The Battle of Chalôns, by Jordanes (6th century CE)
Read about Attila on page 167 in the paragraph that begins "Forty years later . . ."
What words did the writer use to describe Attila's "torture"? _____
Now read the historian Jordanes's description of the Battle of Chalôns, between Romans and Attila in 451 CE.

> Inflamed by [Attila's] words the [Huns] . . . dashed into . . . battle. Hand to hand they clashed . . . the fight grew fierce, confused, monstrous . . . a fight [unlike any] . . . ever recorded. [A] brook flowing . . . through the [battlefield] was greatly increased by blood . . . and [the wounded] . . . drank [its]water. At dawn . . . fields were piled high with corpses . . . and in this most famous [battle], 160,000 men are said to have been slain on both sides.

1. What word does Jordanes used that is the same as the word used in the writing on page 167?

2. What do you think the two authors want the reader to understand about Attila and the Huns?

3. What does the word "monstrous" mean in the description of the battle? (Check more than one.)
   ____ horrible ____ monsters ____ unfair ____ over a large area

4. What happened at the brook flowing through the battlefield?

5. Now reread page 167. Why do you think Pope Leo "begged Attila to spare Rome"?

CHAPTER 26

THE EMPIRE, DIVIDED AND DEFEATED: THE FALL OF ROME/EPILOGUE

CHAPTER SUMMARY

The Roman Empire collapsed in 476 CE after two centuries of decline, but its legacy remains powerful in the modern world.

ACCESS

Now that you have come to the end of this book, you probably know a great deal more about Rome than you once did. You may also have mixed feelings about the empire. In some ways, of course, it was one of the greatest civilizations in the ancient world. In other ways, it was an empire built through bloodshed and conflict In your history journal, write a four line poem with each line starting with a letter in the word R-O-M-E.

CAST OF CHARACTERS

Write why each one was important.

Theodosius _____

Diocletian _____

Odoacer _____

WORD BANK

magnificent   et cetera   circus   monuments   auditorium   video   Vandals   horrified   Renaissance (REN-uh-sahns)

Complete the paragraph below with words from the Word Bank. One word is not used. Circle the word that is not used and write a sentence using it.

Roman citizens were _____ when the barbarian _____ invaded and destroyed their city. The once- _____ civilization fell into ruin for more than 1,000 years. Finally, in the 15th century, a reawakening of interest in Roman culture, the _____, honored the great achievements of the Roman empire. Today the ancient city of Rome still remains, and the influence of Rome is found around the world in architecture, government, and especially in language. From Latin, we have the words for _____, a circular area for entertainment. Another area where people can be heard, an _____, is found in most schools. The word _____, from the verb "to see," comes directly from Latin. So does _____, which means "and so on."

What's the abbreviation for one of the words above? _____

THE ANCIENT ROMAN WORLD   **61**

WITH A PARENT OR PARTNER

In your journal, write as many words that begin with *audio* and *video* as you can think of in one minute. For extra fun, ask a parent or family member or partner to make a list too. Compare lists by reading aloud. Look up any words you don't know.

DO THE MATH

How many years passed between the legendary founding of Rome in 753 BCE and the fall of Rome in 476 CE? _____

CRITICAL THINKING

The sentences below describe the Roman Empire after it divided into two parts. Make a Venn diagram with two circles. Copy the sentences in the correct circles. Any sentences that describe both empires belong in the shaded area where two circles overlap.

- longer borders
- capital: Rome
- larger population
- spoke Latin
- ruled by emperor
- corrupt aristocrats
- Christian
- controlled Egypt
- agricultural economy
- larger army
- capital: Constantinople
- private armies
- manufacturing economy
- trade with Asia

EPILOGUE

WORKING WITH PRIMARY SOURCES

Rutilius Numantius (413 CE)

Read Roma's words in the second paragraph of page 168. What does she mean by "change in old age is humiliating"? _____

The Greatness of Rome in the Days of Ruin

> O Rome, whose place is amongst the stars! . . . Through your temples we draw near to the very heaven. For who can live and forget you?

Compare what Roma says about "religion" with the poet's words about "temples."

WHAT HAPPENED WHEN?
BUILDING A TIMELINE

Looking at your answer for the math challenge above, you can see that the Roman Empire lasted for centuries. For a final project, go back to all the timelines you have made in your history journal. Combine them into one big timeline that shows all the important events. Mark off your timeline in hundreds of years. Write four or five major events each hundred years. Begin at 1000 BCE, when the Trojans arrived on the Italian peninsula. End with 500 CE. Write the events with different colored pens, pencils or other markers to show the change from Etruscan kings, to the Republic, to the Empire, to the conversions of the emperors to Christianity.

REPORTS AND SPECIAL PROJECTS

There's always more to find out about ancient Rome. Take a look at the Further Reading section at the end of the book (pages 180–181). Here you'll find a number of books on different topics relating to ancient Rome. Many of them will be available in your school or local public library.

GETTING STARTED

Explore the Further Reading section for any of these reasons.

— You're curious and want to learn more about a particular topic.

— You want to do a research report on ancient Rome.

— You still have questions about something covered in the book.

— You need more information for a special classroom project.

What's the best way to find the books that will help you the most?

LOOK AT THE SUBHEADS

The books are organized by topic. The subhead Biography tells you where to find books about the lives of the emperors, for example. Go to Science and Technology for books about engineering and other advances Rome introduced. Let the subheads give you ideas for reports and special projects.

LOOK AT THE BOOK TITLES

The titles of the books can tell you a lot about what's inside. The books listed under Military will give you a good picture of army life in ancient Rome, for example. See titles for books about the Roman fort, daily life as a soldier, and Caesar's career as a general.

LOOK FOR GENERAL REFERENCES

This section also lists general books, which are useful starting points for further research. General Works on Ancient Rome will list titles that provide a broad overview of Roman history. Judge by the titles which books will be the most useful to you. Other references include:

— Dictionaries

— Encyclopedias

— Atlases

OTHER RESOURCES

Information comes in all kinds of formats. Use the book to learn about primary sources. Go to the library for videos, DVDs, and audio materials. And don't forget about the Internet!

ANCIENT LITERATURE

Some books listed here include primary sources—see the titles marked by quotation marks. Flip through the book and make a list of primary sources in the text. You can easily find translations of many of these in your school or local library. Think up your own writing projects based on this material. For example, try writing a poem or myth in the same style as an ancient Roman writer. Or get a group together and write a play about Rome. Decide if it will be a tragedy or a comedy. Assign each other different roles, and put on a performance for your class.

AUDIO-VISUAL MATERIALS

Your school or local library can offer documentary videos and DVDs on ancient Rome, as well as audio materials. If you have access to a computer, explore the sites listed on the section titled Websites (page 182) for some good jumping-off points. These are organized by topic, with brief descriptions of what you'll find on the site. Many websites list additional reading, as well as other Internet links you can visit.

What you've found out about ancient Rome so far is just a beginning. Learn more to be part of an ongoing adventure!

NAME _____

LIBRARY / MEDIA CENTER RESEARCH LOG

DUE DATE _____

What I Need to Find

Places I Know to Look

Brainstorm: Other Sources and Places to Look

I need to use:
- ☐ primary sources.
- ☐ secondary

WHAT I FOUND

Title/Author/Location (call # or URL)

	Book/Periodical	Website	Other		Primary Source	Secondary Source		Suggestion	Library Catalog	Browsing	Internet Search	Web link		helpful	relevant
	☐	☐	☐		☐	☐		☐	☐	☐	☐	☐		___	___
	☐	☐	☐		☐	☐		☐	☐	☐	☐	☐		___	___
	☐	☐	☐		☐	☐		☐	☐	☐	☐	☐		___	___
	☐	☐	☐		☐	☐		☐	☐	☐	☐	☐		___	___
	☐	☐	☐		☐	☐		☐	☐	☐	☐	☐		___	___
	☐	☐	☐		☐	☐		☐	☐	☐	☐	☐		___	___

How I Found it   **Rate each source from 1 (low) to 4 (high) in the categories below**

www.ingramcontent.com/pod-product-compliance
Lightning Source LLC
LaVergne TN
LVHW080251260326
834688LV00042BA/1217